Foetal Alcohol Disorders:
Parenting a Child with an Invisible Disability

Julia Brown and Dr Mary Mather

First published in August 2014.

©2013 Julia Brown and Mary Mather
The moral right of Julia Brown and Mary Mather to be identified as the authors of this book has been asserted.

Jacket design and illustrations by Liz O'Donnell
©2014 Liz O'Donnell

Edited by Sarah Giles

Foreword by Simon Brown

ISBN-13 978-1500851880
ISBN-10 1500851884

Foetal Alcohol Spectrum Disorders:
Parenting a Child with an Invisible Disability

Julia Brown and Dr Mary Mather

Foreword by Simon Brown

Illustrated by Liz O'Donnell

Contents

	Foreword by Simon Brown	7
1	The unpredictable impact of alcohol on the developing brain	9
2	Making a diagnosis of FASD	13
3	The lifelong impact of exposure to prenatal alcohol	17
4	FASD, Adoption and foster care	24
5	What does not work and why	34
6	What does work: how to parent the FASD Child	40
7	Sensory processing problems and behaviour	49
8	Eating	57
9	Sleep - and the lack of it!	62
10	Crying, anger, aggression, temper tantrums and meltdowns	69
11	Communication	78
12	Praise, reward, consequences and discipline	90
13	Arrested social development and the problems it causes	100
14	Friendships, social life and recreation	115

15	The major problems of time, money and mathematics	126
16	Education matters	133
17	Becoming independent	138
18	Final word to parents	147
	Further information	152

Foreword

When Dr Mary Mather suggested writing this book to my wife, Julia, over lunch at a conference they were both speaking at here in Oxford, I was very pleased as we were becomingly increasingly aware of the number of parents and carers seeking pragmatic suggestions as they parented children affected by Foetal Alcohol Spectrum Disorders (FASD). This book, therefore, is intended specifically to provide "every day" strategies for all who care for the children affected by FASD, to understand and respond to their child's difficulties.

Wider support in society and from statutory services for these children and their families at the time of writing is still at an early stage in the United Kingdom, but we will continue to strive to improve this, especially via our work at The FASD Trust. One of the key things the Trust is doing is working to increase professional knowledge and better understanding of this invisible but disabling condition.

As father to two children with FASD, I am very aware that there is no 'right' way to parent a child with FASD; each child is unique and their complex problems do not have simple and quick solutions. However, those affected by FASD can achieve.

Improved knowledge is always the key to successful parenting. Mary, Julia - and myself - hope that this book will be a contributing factor in providing parents/carers with more information, empowering them to parent with confidence and bringing them hope for their child's future

Simon Brown
Oxford – July 2014

1 The unpredictable impact of alcohol on the developing brain

Alcohol is a *teratogen*. This means that it is a substance which, taken in pregnancy, can damage the foetus. Worldwide, alcohol is now the leading cause of non-genetic birth defects and brain damage in children. Tragically this damage is also totally preventable. Children born to mothers who have not drunk alcohol will not be affected; it is not "hereditary", passing from one generation to the next.

When a pregnant woman drinks alcohol, it quickly reaches the foetus. The placenta does not provide a barrier because the alcohol molecule is small and easily crosses the placenta. Alcohol can seriously damage the foetus at every stage of pregnancy and the impact is particularly serious for the developing brain. Whereas the other major organs develop mainly in the first three months, the brain continues to develop throughout pregnancy. Alcohol in pregnancy can also structurally damage the **eyes, heart** and **limbs**. Both physical deformities and organic brain damage result. Alcohol can usually affect the foetus in ways that are not physically or immediately obvious.

The degree of damage to the unborn baby will depend on its stage of development at the time of exposure to alcohol because different parts of the brain develop at different times during pregnancy. It will also depend upon how much the mother drinks during pregnancy. There is no evidence of a 'safe' drinking level during pregnancy. However as the amount of alcohol which is consumed by the mother increases, so does the amount of damage inflicted on the baby. The impact will also depend upon the pattern of the mother's drinking. A single drink once a week spaced over a number of hours will have a different effect on the foetus than drinking large amounts over small periods of time, or drinking constantly over a number of days. The British tendency for women to binge drink is thought to be particularly damaging. Each child therefore will have an individual pattern of strengths and weaknesses.

Terminology

Parents can find the large number of diagnostic terms used to describe these children very confusing. They include:

Foetal Alcohol Syndrome (FAS)
Foetal Alcohol Effects (FAE)
Partial Foetal Alcohol Syndrome (PFAS)
Alcohol Related Birth Defects (ARBD)
Alcohol Related Neurodevelopmental Disorder (ARND)
Foetal Alcohol Spectrum Disorder (FASD)

This confusion has arisen because medically our understanding of the complex impact of alcohol on the unborn child has been developing slowly over the last 40 years. Different countries have used different diagnostic terms. Some doctors and researchers have tried to separate the children into groups based on specific characteristics. If you have been given any of these diagnoses by a doctor then your child has been affected by exposure to alcohol before birth. The terms do not describe the severity of their problems.

The spelling of foetus/foetal also varies across the world. Fetus/fetal are the most common spellings and parents are advised to use these when searching for resources on the Internet. In Britain the spelling foetal is more usual.

Throughout this book, the term Foetal Alcohol Spectrum Disorder (FASD) will be used. This is an umbrella term which is increasingly used to describe the whole range of lifelong disabilities which can result from a mother's use of alcohol during pregnancy.

2 Making a diagnosis of FASD

In the USA and Canada, the diagnostic process is a multi-disciplinary one, involving geneticists, paediatricians, psychologists, speech and language therapists, occupational therapists and social workers.

Although, knowledge about the disorder is steadily increasing in the United Kingdom, it can still be very difficult for parents to find a doctor who is prepared to diagnose FASD. Multi-disciplinary diagnosis does not yet exist in most parts of this country.

There is no specific test or investigation and the guidelines for diagnosis vary from country to country. The diagnosis is usually based on a scaled rating of the following four factors:

1. A confirmed history of exposure to alcohol during pregnancy.

2. A pattern of distinct facial features.

3. Poor growth before and after birth: children with FASD are small children who become small adults. Adequate nutrition and a caring

environment are not enough to reverse the growth failure.

4. Brain dysfunction which causes lifelong learning, emotional and behavioural problems.

Each of the criteria will now be discussed in more detail.

Exposure to alcohol

Establishing the history of alcohol consumption in pregnancy is one of the most difficult issues in diagnosis. The pregnant woman who consumes alcohol is not always easily identified. Mothers usually are not forthright about their drinking habits nor are they necessarily able to recall the precise quantities and timing of their drinks. This history is however pivotal in making a diagnosis.

In addition, many children who have been exposed to alcohol in pregnancy are not living with their birth families. At the time concerns are raised about the child, a significant number will have been placed with adopters or foster carers and the exact history of the birth mother's drinking patterns in pregnancy is unknown. Accurate pre-natal information is often sketchy, inaccurately recorded or, even worse, omitted on the spurious grounds of protecting confidentiality.

Facial abnormalities

No single facial feature is diagnostic of FAS. The characteristic features are short palpebral fissures (small eyes), a thin upper lip and a smooth philtrum. The philtrum is the area of the face between the nose and the upper lip. It normally has a prominent 'Cupid's bow' indentation but is flat in the child with FAS. The facial features are best assessed by computer analysis of a digital photograph of the child's face and this technology is being increasing used by some centres in the UK.

However, facial features can be confusing. They only occur if the mother drinks at the beginning of pregnancy when the face is forming. After the face is formed, the features will not occur. In addition, if the mother binge drinks and is sober during this early period, her baby's face will be completely normal. Alcohol however continues to damage the brain throughout pregnancy if the mother continues to drink. It is quite possible for a child to have serious alcohol-induced developmental and behavioural problems with a completely normal face. This is why the history of the mother's alcohol consumption in pregnancy is so important in diagnosis.

In the most severely affected children, the facial features of FAS can be seen at birth. However, the characteristic facial features are most obvious between eight months and eight years of age. As the child approaches adolescence, the typical facial features become less pronounced. In some adults, facial characteristics have become so normal that early childhood photographs must be used to confirm diagnosis.

As well as the facial features, alcohol can affect the development of any organ in the body. Other alcohol related birth defects include abnormalities in heart, bone, muscle, kidney, eye and ear defects. These additional defects occur in about 30 per cent of affected children.

Neurodevelopmental and behavioural problems

Prenatal alcohol exposure can produce a whole spectrum of dysfunctions on the developing central nervous system that manifest in a range of effects from subtle to severe and persist throughout the life span. These neuropsychological problems include hyperactivity, impulsiveness, short memory span, difficulty concentrating, poor planning and organisational skills, poor judgement and failure to consider consequences, motor difficulties, speech and language difficulties, perceptual disorders and specific learning disabilities. These will be described in more detail in the next chapter.

3 The lifelong impact of exposure to prenatal alcohol

The main burden of caring for children affected by alcohol is caused by their long-term problems with learning, language, and behaviour. The pattern of these difficulties changes as the child moves from infancy to adulthood. The impact of the damage presents in different ways at different ages. It is important to stress, however, that these difficulties are all caused by brain damage before birth.

British health and social care professionals have been slow to accept that there can be a direct link between behaviour and pre-birth organic brain damage. Professional practice, especially in social work, has been dominated by attachment theory and the impact of post-birth trauma, neglect and abuse. This lack of understanding has led to many parents and carers being unfairly blamed for their child's problems and then given the wrong strategies for managing them.

Infants with FASD are often tremulous and irritable. They have a weak sucking reflex and low muscle tone. They have major feeding difficulties and are often uninterested in food. Feeding can take hours. Despite adequate nutrition, the child gains weight very slowly. The children are frequently referred to hospital for investigation of their poor weight gain or failure to thrive. They have erratic sleep patterns with no predictable sleep-wake cycle.

As toddlers, the lack of interest in food, slow weight gain and disrupted sleep pattern continues. The children are slow to achieve their developmental milestones. They can be hypersensitive to noise, bright lights, temperature and touch. The children are very social but over-friendly and indiscriminate with relationships. They can be excessively talkative. They have a short attention span and are easily distractible and often hyperactive. They tend to "flit" from one thing to another with 'butterfly-like' movements. They are unable to comprehend danger and do not respond well to verbal warnings. They are prone to temper tantrums and non-compliance. They do not respond well to changes and prefer routine. The gap between the alcohol-affected child and their peers steadily widens as the child gets older.

It is often when the child starts school that the problems become noticeable. Compared to their peers, the affected child's motor skills are poor, uncoordinated and clumsy. They have problems with fine motor skills, handwriting, fastening buttons, zips and shoe laces. They find it difficult to wait for their turn, to follow rules or to cooperate. They often interrupt the work and play of others and are inappropriately intrusive. They have poor peer relations and can become socially isolated, preferring to play with younger children or adults rather than with their peer group.

During the first two years in school, most will achieve some basic reading and writing skills and the extent of any learning delay may not be initially apparent. Mathematics and numeracy, however, are always problem areas. The affected children are often very mathematically disabled.

Attention deficits and poor impulse control become more apparent as the demands for classroom attention increase. The child is unable to transfer learning from one situation to another and to learn from experience. The child has a very poor memory needing constant repetition and reminders for even basic activities at home and school. Their skills in school can often fluctuate from day to day, giving the mistaken impression that their poor performance is deliberate. Information is learned, retained for a while and then lost. They exist in the 'here and now', lacking an internal clock and are unable to monitor their own work or behaviour.

As they progress through school, reading and spelling skills usually reach their peak. The children have increasing difficulty maintaining their attention, completing assignments and mastering new academic skills. As they are usually very concrete thinkers, they have trouble working with ideas. They tend to fall further behind peers as the world becomes increasingly abstract and concept based. They struggle to understand time and money and find it difficult to identify and label emotions and feelings.

The children often have good verbal skills, a superficially friendly social manner and obvious good intentions which mask the seriousness of the problem. They talk too much and too quickly but have little to communicate. They like to be the centre of attention and their outgoing and friendly manner, which is often seen as positive in early childhood, becomes more problematic as the child grows older. They are increasingly seen as immature and naïve.

The children are frequently misjudged as being lazy, stubborn and unwilling to learn. They may tell you that they understand your instructions, but then are unable to carry them out. They have learned to act as though they understand, but cannot follow a series of actions through by themselves. Their logic is faulty because they lack critical thinking and judgement skills. They have increasing problems with abstract thinking and are unable to link cause and effect. They are unable to apply previously learnt rules to a new situation. A high degree of impulsivity and a total lack of inhibition mean the children are easily influenced and subject to peer manipulation and exploitation. They have difficulty showing remorse or taking responsibility for actions, and frequently behave in ways that place themselves or others at risk. They are at high risk for problems with the law and involvement in the criminal justice system.

As the children mature into adolescence and adulthood, the facial deformities become less noticeable but the short stature and microcephaly (small head) remain. Educational achievement can be extremely limited. Lack of comprehension, judgement and attention skills cause adults affected by pre-natal alcohol to experience major psychosocial and adjustment problems for the rest of their lives. They have difficulty holding down jobs, problems managing money, poor social skills, low motivation and may become increasingly withdrawn and isolated. Antisocial behaviour and inability to live independently are common.

Strengths

Some of the characteristic behaviours associated with FASD should also be seen as strengths. It is important to recognise and reinforce these strengths, which will increase the child's confidence and self-esteem. They can be used as strategies for education and behaviour management. The positives reported by all the parents include the following:

- Creative intelligence (e.g. artistic, musical)
- Perseverance (determined, persistent, willing, committed hard workers, involved, energetic)
- Highly moral, deep sense of fairness, rigid belief systems
- Strong sense of self
- Friendly, trusting
- Loyal, loving
- Affectionate, compassionate, gentle
- Tactile, cuddly
- Concerned, sensitive
- Love children, animals, nurturing, enjoy gardening and cooking
- Highly verbal with a rich fantasy life, often wonderful story tellers

- Exceptionally good long-term visual memory
- Spontaneous, have lots of energy
- Curious and questioning, have a great sense of wonder

Multiple diagnoses

Children with FASD often accumulate multiple diagnoses over time. None of these diagnoses is necessarily wrong but essentially all of them fail to recognise the origins of the problem. Unfortunately, rather than clarifying the situation, these multiple diagnoses often contribute to confusion and fragmentation. They often generate inappropriate and ineffective interventions which concentrate on the behavioural symptoms rather than the cause. Misdiagnosis frequently leads to the imposition of intervention strategies that fail. Multiple misdiagnoses are confusing and depressing for parents and the net result is a downward spiral in the child's mental and social health and their family functioning.

The children often meet the criteria for attention deficit disorder, autism and attachment disorder, dyspraxia, learning difficulties, post-traumatic stress disorder, auditory or visual processing problems or a conduct disorder. This is because they can show symptoms of all these problems. None however fully explain the totality of the child's problems or the challenge of living with them.

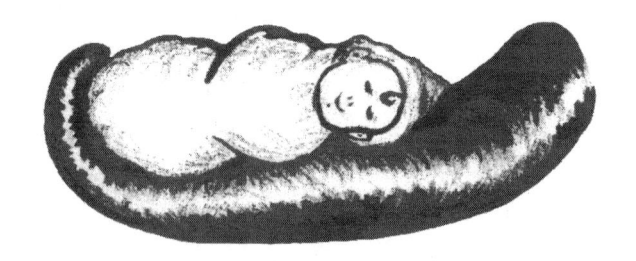

4   FASD, adoption and foster care

Alcohol, drugs or both?

Many children for whom alternative carers are sought have been exposed to both drugs and alcohol. Information about parental drug use is often readily available to potential carers whereas the parent's alcohol misuse is often ignored or unknown.

Problem drug use in the UK is characterised by the use of multiple drugs, often by injection, and is strongly associated with alcohol misuse. Drug and alcohol abusing parents usually smoke heavily, have poor diets and live in conditions of extreme socio-economic deprivation. All these factors make their unborn babies very vulnerable.

The strategies in this book will usually help most children, even those not exposed to drugs and alcohol. All children respond to consistency, predictability and routine. So if you are caring for a child exposed to drugs, where the alcohol history is not known, try them to see if they work. Keep the ones which help and abandon those which do not help your child. Parents often find that they need to try a number of different strategies before they find the one that works for their child.

All children are unique. It is still not possible to determine precisely which children will be affected by parental substance abuse and in what way. Not all children prenatally exposed to drugs and alcohol will have long-term problems. Some appear to have minimal or no apparent problems whilst others have very severe problems and there is a spectrum of difficulties between these two extremes.

Rule 1: Get all the information that you can

We all need comprehensive and detailed knowledge about our children in order to parent them sensitively and effectively. In addition to the usual roles which all parents undertake, substitute carers frequently have to uncover, discover or simply guess about the past and its continuing influence on the future of their child. Only then can they help their children to repair, rebuild or compensate for what has gone before.

No one should ever be asked to parent a child in the absence of **all** the information that is available to professionals about the child. Foster and adoptive parents need to be archaeologists of a child's past before they can be the architects of the child's future.

Comprehensive identification and assessment of problems is likely to facilitate a placement rather than threaten it. Substitute carers require a very honest assessment of the difficulties they are likely to face in meeting a child's needs. Carers must seek every opportunity to obtain as much health and social information as possible about a prospective child. They need to ask questions, ask them repeatedly and, if necessary, make a nuisance of themselves to get the answers.

Introductions can be a tense and fraught time for all concerned. The potential carers, who have undergone a long assessment process and potentially endured a long wait, may feel their lives have been 'on hold' for months. The social worker, who may have been involved in extended legal proceedings, can be equally anxious for a vulnerable child to move quickly into a permanent placement. The process can become rushed and events move at breakneck speed. In addition to the excitement of a long awaited child, carers are often organising or renovating family homes, tying up loose ends at work in preparation for leave and undertaking tiring journeys to the child's foster family. Additional information, particularly in a superficially healthy child, may not seem a very important issue. In this heady atmosphere many of the questions formulated during the assessment are left unasked, only to be regretted later.

Rule 2: Pre-placement health assessments must be comprehensive

The assessment of the child must provide an accurate and realistic picture of physical health, developmental, behavioural and emotional needs. Children affected by drugs and/or alcohol should not have a pre-placement medical examination done by a doctor who **only** conducts a physical examination. A comprehensive family medical history and the personal medical history of the child is essential.

Health is not just the absence of illness, preventative health is also important. Vision, hearing, dental checks and immunisations matter and depending on the age of the child must be done before placement. It is advisable for children with particularly complex or subtle problems to be examined by a community consultant paediatrician or by an experienced agency medical adviser.

For a child who is brought up within his or her birth family, there is little need to depend on accurate medical record-keeping. Most birth parents have an intimate knowledge of their own child's health and development. For children separated from their families the loss or delay in the transfer of medical records, disrupted medical histories and inadequate record-keeping is all too common.

A child's medical history starts before conception when the genetic material of both parents is combined to form a new and unique individual. Genetics in substitute care is far from straightforward. Huge information gaps often exist. The family tree may be complicated and tortuous. The mother may be unwilling to divulge the father's identity, or they may disappear during the legal proceedings.

A child's medical history continues through pregnancy, delivery and the early neonatal period. Pre-birth traumas can include the exposure to violence (including attempted abortion), feelings of ambivalence, rejection or grief in the mother, maternal illness or poor nutrition in addition to the abuse of tobacco, alcohol and drugs.

It is important that adopters have full information about the child's birth. Not only should this include information such as the hospital where the child was born and the child's birth weight, but also the child's head circumference at birth because this is an important measure of prenatal brain growth. Any possible areas of distress to the infant that occurred around the time of delivery must be documented. These include instrumental deliveries, caesarean section, prolonged labours, time spent in the special care baby unit and prolonged separation from the mother. Some children may have had repeated or extended early separations from their birth mother.

Postnatal depression can make mothers emotionally unavailable to their babies. Many children are subjected to inappropriate attempts at rehabilitation, or may have spent periods of time in a drug withdrawal unit.

Early childhood experiences, the arrival of siblings, common childhood illnesses, admissions to hospital, accidents, exposure to the effects of poverty, deprivation and abuse all complete important pieces of information to a child's medical history.

Carers need to ensure that they see a full record of the child's medical history. They should be assertive in their requests to discuss any questions or concerns with the specialists involved with the child. For example, if the child has ever received a psychological or psychiatric assessment, the prospective parents should be given a copy of the report. If the child has been tested for HIV or hepatitis B and C, any prospective carers should make sure that the implications of the test results are explained to them in simple, unambiguous terms.

Health is always more than just physical health. Children are always growing and developing and reports from nursery or classroom teachers give essential information about a child's developmental skills, particularly in the social context. When appropriate, adopters should always ask to speak to a health visitor, teacher or other key figure who knows the child in a context outside the foster home. They should request medical and developmental information about the siblings if children are not to be placed together and the reasons for separation.

A very important and frequently forgotten point is that a child's family history does not stop with his or her permanent placement. It must be kept up-to-date. Family members may die or develop serious illnesses, which may be of genetic significance, and siblings can develop a number of health or learning problems. Sadly many drug- and alcohol-abusing parents will not live long enough for their child to be able to contact them in adult life. Any information about a deceased parent is valuable to a child but it is important that the information children receive is not purely negative. A pen picture of their parents before they became entrenched drug or alcohol addicts is often forgotten but can paint a completely different picture for a child in the future.

Unfortunately, there is currently no 'laboratory test' that confirms whether or not a child has FASD. Diagnosis is a clinical judgement based on assessment of the child with regard to specific symptoms and criteria. The following will help a professional to make a diagnosis although sadly this information is often missing in adopted and fostered children.

1. A medical history to include the mother's illnesses, drinking pattern, drug and tobacco use during pregnancy.

2. The child's birth and health history (birth weight, developmental milestones).

3. The placement history.

4. Any assessments by other professionals

5. The records of the child growth (height, weight and head circumference) over the years.

6. Any siblings known to have FASD or other alcohol-related birth defects.

7. A list of 'problem' areas in social, behavioural and adaptive functioning.

Rule 3: Do not let yourself be overburdened

Alcohol-dependent mothers frequently have large families. As their alcohol dependence gets worse over time, the amount of alcohol that each child is exposed to in pregnancy increases. The youngest children in these families are frequently the most seriously affected. It is quite common in our experience for adopters to be caring for sibling groups all of whom have FASD. This is because social workers have a duty to place siblings together whenever possible. The needs of these children become more complex as they grow and develop. The new baby they have been asked to take may have few or no problems initially, but the carers can find themselves coping with more and more difficult issues as their family gets older.

Do not be afraid to say 'no' to the request to take a sibling. Every family has its breaking point and only you know how much your family can manage. Talk to other adopters caring for school-aged and older children before you make your decision. Talk about post-adoption support. There may not be any additional resources for a newly born baby and then you will have to fight for help later when all the social workers have moved on and you may be living in a different region from the birth family. Consider the social and financial impact on your family if a child's need extended care into adult life.

Rule 4: Coming to terms with reality

Caring for a child disabled by alcohol exposure arouses strong emotions. Birth mothers will feel very guilty. Other members of the extended family may feel very angry. All carers must come to terms with their sense of loss and the realisation of what might have been. After the initial stages of grief and anger however, most parents and carers will develop a strong desire to 'fix' the problem and to make everything all right. This understandable desire to fix things can get in the way of helping the child.

Everyone caring for the child must accept that there is no cure. This is a lifelong condition and one which must be managed and not solved. Whilst every effort should be made to enable the child to reach their full potential, this must be tempered with an acceptance that the potential may be very limited. We need strategies, not solutions, where creative support enables the affected child to become a contributing member of society.

5 What does not work and why

Before discussing those strategies and parenting methods that will work, it is important to mention those which do **not** help the alcohol-affected child. Unfortunately, the most unsuccessful strategies are traditional parenting techniques. These are the strategies that are often taught on parenting courses and found in most parenting manuals.

Alcohol-affected children do not respond like typically developing children. Behaviour due to organic brain disease cannot be changed easily. Children with FASD do learn, but they learn differently. They need structure, routine, repetition and constant supervision to achieve success. Even the most experienced parents will feel a sense of 'failure' when the wrong strategies are used.

Traditional behaviour management consists essentially of rewarding 'good' behaviour and ignoring the 'bad' to effect change. For these techniques to work however, the child must understand cause and effect, must have some understanding of the impact of their behaviour on others and must have some concept of 'future earning'. The child must understand that behaving in the right way now will bring a reward in the future. The alcohol-affected child does not have these skills.

Stickers, tokens, and star charts do not work. This is because affected children do not learn from their mistakes. They live in the moment and accept life as it happens. They have no concept of time and a poor memory. The sticker given as a reward on Monday, is forgotten by Wednesday and certainly has no impact by Friday. For the same reasons, taking things away and cancelling future trips or treats is unlikely to be successful.

Strategies such as time out and grounding will also fail. The alcohol-affected child often has a very impaired concept of time and has literally has no idea if the time out period is long or short. Time out is unlikely to prevent a behaviour recurring, will not produce any useful learning and could make behaviour worse.

Problems with sensory overload lead to large emotional outbursts which the child may not know how to stop. A naughty step or chair will not help the child to self-regulate and calm down. Instead find a place that is comfortable and quiet. It might be the child's bedroom or in a room away from other household activities. The most important thing is to significantly reduce the stress the child is feeling from noise and chaos. This comfort corner, which is not a punishment zone, might have a squashy bean bag, a soft quilt, subdued lighting and headphones playing favourite soothing music. Removing the child from the situation and giving them a tool for controlling outbursts in the future is more likely to be successful. The child will usually tell you when they are feeling calm enough to return to family life.

Using money as a reward is also unhelpful. Understanding money and making other contracts with a child requires abstract thinking skills. For these strategies to work, the child needs to have a concept of the value of money, understand that an amount of money will only last a certain amount of time depending upon how much you spend and realise that impulsive spending uses all your money in one go.

Often the so-called 'naughty' behaviour of the child is due to an inability to control their impulses. They see something, they like it, they touch it and take it. They have no concept of ownership or property. No one is holding the object they want, it is just sitting on a shelf in shop or supermarket, so how can it 'belong' to someone else? They are then further confused when an adult uses abstract language in a complex sentence such as 'you should not take something which belongs to someone else'. (More of abstract language later!)

To the great distress of many families, the bizarre behaviours which alcohol-affected children can develop are often mistakenly blamed on the child's parents or the family environment. In a misguided attempt to help the family, the parents are then sent on a traditional parenting course. When the parents attempt to follow the techniques they have been taught, implementation is at best a complete failure and at worst, makes the family situation worse. The parent is then blamed for not implementing the techniques properly rather than the technique itself being seen as wrong and unhelpful.

Another solution frequently offered to the child and family offered are so-called 'talking therapies'. These do not work with the alcohol-affected child. The children have a poor understanding of complex verbal language, particularly abstract language which involves talking about feelings. They have impaired memories. They are unable to sequence events and unable to understand time. They often become confused and fearful. When the therapist talks about a behaviour which has occurred in the past, for example sexual abuse, the child can think that this is the behaviour that they should be displaying now. The wrong therapeutic approach, combined with the child's difficulty in grasping concepts and understanding emotions, only adds to their confusion and unhappiness. Similarly, life story work with adopted and fostered children is often of limited value because of the child's difficulty with memory and understanding timeframes.

Finally, being punitive will always fail. Verbal threats and physical punishment do not work for any child. Sadly, society can be punitive to the carers of alcohol-affected children because the behaviour of the child is so bizarre and difficult to understand. We are aware of carers who have been threatened with the removal of their child or even had a child removed from them because of the child's behaviour.

Nearly all the parents that we have met have been sent on a traditional parenting course. They have usually attended these courses under duress, very conscious of partially veiled threats about the removal of their child and too frightened to refuse.

Traditional behaviour management courses do not work but the parents are by then understandably reluctant to be honest about how little the family situation has changed. They keep the seriousness of their concerns to themselves and are more reluctant to ask for help in the future. It must be constantly borne in mind that a child exposed to alcohol before birth is biologically affected. They have organic brain disease which environmental factors can improve but not cure. Removing a child to a new set of carers will not cure organic brain damage. Subjecting the family to child protection procedures will fail. Even therapeutic foster care will not work unless the carers have been very specifically trained.

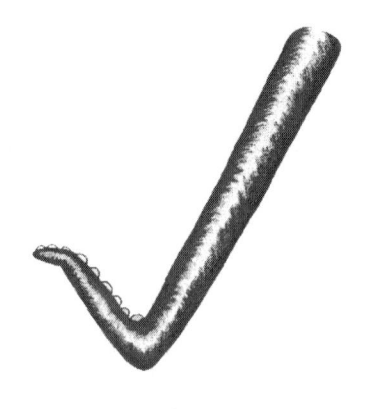

6 What does work: how to parent the FASD child

The following general strategies will help all alcohol-affected children; strategies for more specific behavioural problems will be discussed in later chapters. There are however a number of key guidelines in managing behaviour. It is important to remember however that all children, alcohol-affected or not, are first and foremost individuals with distinct personalities, preferences, and temperaments. Parenting tips which may work wonders with one child may prove inappropriate and ineffective for another.

Owning the diagnosis

Professor Ann Streissguth, who is based at the University of Washington, Seattle, USA, has carried out detailed research over 40 years following the developmental outcomes for a large group of people affected by prenatal alcohol. One of her earliest findings was that those children who do best have a clear diagnosis. Being diagnosed before the age of 6, and being told your diagnosis in an age-appropriate way which you can understand, was associated with the best outcomes. If a child 'owns' their disability and is clearly able to articulate it, the outcomes for them as adults are more positive.

Sharing the diagnosis with a child is not easy and it can be particularly heart-breaking for a birth mother. The FASD Trust has produced a set of books and computer apps for children, young people, their caregivers and their friends. These materials, which are constantly being expanded and revised to cover various age groups and retain cultural relevance, seek to explain in a simple way the implications of an FASD diagnosis.

Building up a local network of support for the future

Children affected by FASD need to be surrounded by a community of people who understand them and their needs. Unsurprisingly, another of Prof Streissguth's key findings is that children who are in the same placement or family for as long as possible have the best outcomes. Stability gives a long timeframe for strategies and support networks to be built up. One mother from London described herself as a 'puppet master, pulling all the strings behind the scenes', ensuring that her child was always supported and protected by her local community.

Sharing the diagnosis with the extended family, friends and neighbours is the best starting point for ensuring your child gets the support they need. It can also give parents more opportunities for short breaks. FASD children, who are not obviously disabled, often do not qualify for most of the local authority respite care services available to the parents of children with more obvious and visible disability.

Routines and consistency

The child with FASD thinks differently from other people. A major difference is their inability to learn new behaviours or to learn from the consequences of their actions. This means that children with FASD have difficulty learning even relatively simple routines at home and need constant repetition to learn new things. One of the most important things parents can do for their child is to be very consistent in their daily routine. Develop a schedule and stick to it. If a change in routine is going to occur, explain this to the child in advance and prepare them for it.

Tell the school

Many parents have reported that as long as they can manage their children in the protected, structured, supervised environment of their home, their children can function quite well. Therefore, it comes as no surprise that school is often a major challenge for both child and parent alike. The school environment poses three different types of challenges to children with FASD. First, they will struggle with the curriculum, particularly abstract areas like mathematics. Secondly, schools are by their very nature less structured than home environments. Thirdly, FASD children always struggle with the social aspects of school life.

In the United Kingdom, teachers and educational psychologists have limited knowledge of FASD. Most parents have reported that their first role was that of educator. In particular, they had to try to explain what FASD is, its effects on their children, and implications for learning and behaviour. Even among parents who had a relatively positive experience with their school, there is still a need to advocate for their children. The issue of school is explored a little further in Chapter 16.

Information

Knowledge is power. Parents who do not understand why their child is having so many difficulties doing and learning things that other children do easily are isolated and bewildered. They feel that their family and friends cannot understand what their daily life is like. Even worse, they can feel like a bad parent because other people in society, who do not understand FASD, blame them for their children's difficulties. To know that other parents are having similar problems is a great support. Many of the parents report that the first thing they did when they learned or suspected they had a child with FASD was to educate themselves as much as they could. For many, education has been a continuous process. So join a support group (The FASD Trust run these across the UK) and download some of the excellent resources available on the internet.

Success comes in small uneven steps

Parents need to be patient and calm as well as having reduced and flexible expectations, because, in the words of one parent, 'things the child does well now he may not do well in two weeks' time'. There is very little that is slow and steady about children with FASD. Some days the child will show flashes of promising behaviour that exceed parental expectations. On these good days, a parent is tempted to think that their child does not have FASD or is only mildly affected. At the other extreme, on those days when the child falls short of already lowered expectations, it is easy to despair. The parent starts to imagine all the horror stories they have heard about living with FASD, a nightmare from which their family will never recover.

Inconsistent performance is very common in FASD. Every once in a while, all children will meet or exceed parental expectation. Tragically these fluctuations can reinforce the false belief that the child can do it 'if only they try harder'. In fact the child is trying just as hard on an 'on' day as on an 'off' day and is frequently exhausted with trying and failing. Peaks and valleys in behaviour are normal in FASD. They are to be expected. They are not predictive of potential; they just are. If we cannot manage the brain damage caused by prenatal alcohol exposure, we can manage our expectations and stay sane!

Structure

All children with FASD need to have a very structured environment which includes choices within clear and predictable routines. Try to avoid situations where the child will be over stimulated by people, noise, light or movement. Parents have found some of the following strategies useful.

- Write down or draw a picture of what needs to be done to complete a task. For example, you might put photographs on the bathroom wall doing each step of an activity such as brushing their teeth.

- Break down daily activities into specific steps. Do everything in the same way and in the same order every day (e.g. wake the child in the same predictable way each morning.) This may help the child become more comfortable moving between activities, and able to operate more independently.

- Imitate daily activities in play. Have a place for everything and everything in its place. Allow only one item out at a time.

- Store things together by a system (e.g. by type, size, colour, etc.). This will help the child become more independent. For example, if all the blocks are stored together, the child may learn where to go get them without your assistance.

- Place labels on the outside of drawers, cupboards, shelves, and so on. Use single words or pictures to indicate contents.

- If the child has difficulty understanding boundaries and private spaces, such as shared bedrooms, marking off areas with masking tape may be helpful.

Supervision

As a general rule of thumb, FASD children will have a developmental age which is approximately half their chronological age. They need a level of supervision and parenting appropriate to their developmental age, so that they do not get into trouble or place themselves in dangerous situations. Parents need to maintain a constant high level of supervision even if they are accused of being over-protective and 'not letting their children go'.

Children with FASD have trouble understanding the link between behaviour and consequences. They can be manipulated by older, more streetwise children and they are typically the child in any group who gets caught and blamed, even though they did not initiate or carry out the action.

Parents need to sleep, so keeping the child's bedroom fairly sparse can minimise the potential for disaster! For the child who wanders at night, an alarm on the bedroom door, a gate at the top of the stairs and locks on rooms downstairs might be necessary.

FASD children are frequently friendly and outgoing with little sense of stranger awareness. If the child approaches strangers, deal with it immediately in front of the stranger e.g. 'This is a stranger; this is someone we do not know. We do not talk to people we do not know'. This may be difficult and embarrassing, but it is essential to reinforce the concept immediately.

One major mistake often made by well-meaning professionals is the assumption that now the child is now 14 or 15, they need to be 'more independent'. Ignore this advice! When parents or carers, pressured by society's perception that all young people need to be given freedom in order to be independent, have allowed their children out without adequate supervision, disaster soon follows! Follow your own instincts as to what feels right for your child. Children with FASD must be parented according to their developmental age and not their biological age.

7 Sensory processing problems and behaviour

These problems are very common in children with FASD. Many of them will be diagnosed as having a sensory processing disorder. It is important to stress that this diagnosis does not mean that your child has yet another new and different condition. This term is simply a reflection of the damage in the area of the brain which is responsible for analysing and processing the information which comes from our senses, vision, hearing touch taste, smell and movement. Unrecognised sensory problems cause children to show inexplicable behaviour difficulties which puzzle and distress parents.

Sensory processing (sometimes called sensory integration) is a term that refers to the way the brain receives messages from the senses and turns them into appropriate behavioural responses. A Sensory Processing Disorder (also known as sensory integration dysfunction) exists when sensory signals do not get organised into appropriate responses.

Sensory problems have major implications for a child's ability to carry out a large number of ordinary everyday activities.

Sensory difficulties vary from child to child and are always on a continuum. A sensory processing disorder can affect a child in only one sense; for example, just touch, just sight or just movement, or it can affect multiple senses. Some children over-respond to sensation, while others under-respond. Some children under-respond in one sense and over-respond in another. Other children exhibit an appetite for sensation that seems to be in perpetual overdrive and will seek out sensations incessantly. The problem of overstimulation is often first seen in alcohol-exposed newborns who tend to be anxious, easily upset infants. Some alcohol-affected children remain hypersensitive to sensory stimulation most of their lives.

The main sensory areas are as follows:

Tactile

Tactile refers to the sense of touch. Children who are **hypersensitive** to touch will refuse or resists messy play. They will avoid cuddling and light touch and dislike being kissed. Rough clothes or seams in their socks will distress them. They may be very over sensitive to even a slight change in the temperature of water and quickly become upset in a bath or shower. They will become upset when their hair or nails are cut. Tactile hypersensitivity can result in a child refusing to walk barefoot on grass or a sandy beach. Another child accidentally brushing against their skin can feel like a punch and the FASD child often responds with a harder punch back. At the end of the school day the parent will then be faced with a teacher or another parent complaining about the child's aggressive behaviour without understanding the real reason for the reaction

Children who are **hyposensitive** to touch are often messy unkempt children who may not even realise that their hands or face are dirty. They will touch everything and anything constantly. They do not seem to feel pain. They have no concept of how hard they are pushing against another person or how tightly they are gripping them. The will use an inappropriate amount of force when writing or playing and often tear paper when rubbing out and easily break their possessions.

If your child is hypersensitive to touch, avoid itchy, rough clothing. Soft, loose material is more easily tolerated. Elastic waistbands, sock seams, ties under the chin, labels at the back of the neck, washing tags, jeans seams, appliqués with a scratchy back, hair bands and stiff shoes may cause problems. Solutions include removing tags from clothing, washing new clothes two or three times before wearing and turning socks and gloves with seams inside out.

Vision

Vision refers to sight and the ability to correctly perceive, discriminate, process and respond to what one sees. Children who are **hypersensitive** to light are irritated by sunlight or bright lights. They are easily distracted by light or bright colours. They may avoid eye contact and become over-aroused and anxious in brightly coloured stimulating classrooms with lots of different coloured materials, paintings and displays.

Children who are **hyposensitive** to visual signals will have difficulty controlling their eye movements and tracking objects. They can mix up similar letters. They can focus on small details in a picture and miss the whole. They lose their place frequently when reading or copying from the blackboard. They will take longer to react to changes in their environment. They will fail to notice things going on around them.

When crossing the road they can have difficulty in judging how far away a car is and how fast a car is approaching. These children may need lifelong supervision when crossing roads.

Some babies and toddlers seem very sensitive to bright light. These infants become upset in bright sunlight or when the sun shines in their eyes. They may need to have their cots moved away from the bedroom window, have window blinds fitted and go outside with the hood of the pram up on sunny days. Older children may be upset by bright lights, particularly fluorescent lights. They are more sensitive to the flicker (and the hum) of a fluorescent light than other children. They will turn away from sunlight reflecting from water or snow. They will find sunglasses and tinted glasses (prescription and non-prescription) helpful in reducing glare and may need low or recessed lighting both at home and at school.

Auditory

Auditory sensations relate to sound and an ability to correctly perceive, discriminate, process and respond to sound. Children who are **hypersensitive** to sound will cover their ears and be startled by, or fearful of loud sounds. They can be distracted by sounds not even noticed by others. They can be frightened by toilets flushing, hand dryers, hairdryers, vacuum cleaners, trains or accelerating motor bikes. They may refuse to visit public toilets, the school dining room, restaurants, train or bus station. Loud noises may be quite painful for the child's ears, but use earplugs only under supervision. Loud music is often distracting because it seems to 'switch off' what is being seen visually. It is as though the child can have either visual stimulus or auditory stimulus, but not both at once. If your child is very distressed by noise, avoid crowded situations. Shop in the evening when supermarkets are less crowded. Explain to the school the reason for the child's distress in the dining room or toilet, and see if strategies can be put in place to give the child a quieter environment at school break times.

Children who are **hyposensitive** to sound may not respond to verbal cues. They can appear confused about where a sound is coming from. They often ask 'what?' very frequently. These children are usually referred for repeated hearing tests because they are incorrectly thought to be deaf. These children often love really loud music and make a lot of noise.

Vestibular and Proprioception

These senses relate to movement and balance. Signals from the inner ear continuously inform the brain about balance, gravity and the position of the baby in space, whilst input from the muscles and joints inform the brain about body posture, changes in position, stretch, weight and pressure and movement.

Children who are **hypersensitive** to these signals will avoid playground and moving equipment like escalators and lifts. They will be fearful of heights and afraid of falling. They will dislike being tipped upside down or walking on uneven surfaces. They will avoid rapid, sudden or rotating movements. They have difficulty understanding where body is in relation to other objects. They are clumsy children who are always bumping into things. They can appear stiff and uncoordinated.

Children who are **hyposensitive** to these signals seem to crave any possible movement experience, especially fast or spinning ones. They love trampolines, playground rides or spinning in circles. They never seem to sit still. They are constant thrill seekers. Even when sitting they will repetitively shake their arms and legs. They love being tossed in the air. They never seem to get dizzy. They full of excess energy, constantly jumping, crashing, and running around. They love to be hugged tightly, prefer tight clothing, adore rough play and may be inadvertently aggressive with other children. They are often additionally diagnosed with ADHD.

Taste and smell

These senses allow a child to correctly perceive, discriminate, process and respond to what they are eating and drinking and what is in the mouth. Children who are **hypersensitive** to these signals will be very picky eaters. They will eat a very limited range of foods, may gag on textured food and have difficulty with sucking, chewing, and swallowing.

They will dislike other sensations which arise from the mouth and can be extremely fearful of the dentist. They can dislike the taste or smell of toothpaste and avoid brushing their teeth. They can be upset or even nauseated by certain cooking smells, perfumes or cleaning materials. They may refuse to visit certain places because of the way they smell or choose foods based only on smell.

Children who are **hyposensitive** to these signals will in contrast tend to lick, taste or chew inedible objects, such as pens, pencils or their clothes. They will prefer intensely flavoured foods. They may drool excessively. They will not notice unpleasant or noxious odours and may smell new foods when they are first introduced to them.

Unrecognised sensory problems affecting the mouth, taste and smell will contribute to the feeding difficulties which nearly all FASD children experience. These are covered in more detail in the next chapter.

8 Eating

Eating problems are common in alcohol-affected children. Eating difficulties are a major source of stress for parents. Some children over-eat, some under-eat, some eat very slowly, while others never seem to feel hungry. Many children use food as a comfort. Also, since children with FASD have poor impulse control, mealtime itself can be a problem because the dinner table is full of tempting play things like cutlery, glasses, bottles and condiments as well as food. Anticipate that meals could be a problem and be very flexible in your expectations and approach. Never use food as a "punishment" nor as a "treat" or inducement for good behaviour; make eating food a "habit", a normal part of daily life.

Always remember that children with FASD are often slow to gain weight, despite good nutrition and adequate calories in their diet. Growth failure is part of the wider picture of FASD. The affected child is light at birth, grows slowly in childhood, is often misdiagnosed as failing to thrive and ultimately can become a small adult.

However, if the child starts to lose weight for no obvious reason, or has persistent vomiting or diarrhoea, a medical check-up is always needed. If this happens it is essential that you inform the doctor that the child has been exposed to alcohol before birth.

A child with FASD may eat slowly because of poor muscle control or poor swallowing reflex. Parents need to accept that their child may be a sloppy eater and have a sensitive gag reflex. They may not understand the sensations of hunger or thirst.

Some infants seem not to 'feel' bottle teats or spoons in their mouth. Some have a high palate which stops the mouth closing properly around a teat. This makes bottle feeding slow, inefficient and very tiring for the infant.

Carefully control the temperature and texture of foods according to the individual child. The child may have hypersensitivity toward certain food textures or can be very sensitive to the temperature of food. Bland pureed food without any texture may be rejected. Conversely, some children will reject all lumpy food. Avoid spicy foods for young children if they react to strong flavours. However, some children do not have a distinct taste sense and these children will prefer stronger flavours, like lemon. Always limit or even avoid foods which are high in sugar and food additives.

Try making meal time fun by arranging the food on the plate to make a "happy face" or a "sea" of stew with an "island" of mashed potatoes.

In older children, allow ample time to eat. Establish a firm routine for meals at the table and have clear rules which apply to everyone. For example, the family will all choose what they eat from what is prepared. No one leaves the table without permission; the child must ask to be excused. Insist that the child take at least one bite of everything but have reasonable expectations of portion size.

Manipulating forks and knives may be a continuing problem so allow use of fingers or a spoon, even for older children. Children with FASD tire easily, and even with children aged 5-7 you might need, on occasions, to feed them their evening meal, in the same way you would a much younger child or toddler.

Work on one table manner at a time. Integrate a new 'manner' only when the previous one has been successfully used for some time.

Use the same dishes for the child at every meal. Serve meals at the same time daily. Give the child a specific seat at the table. If the child cannot reach the floor when seated and finds this uncomfortable, allow the child to stand instead or place a stool under the child's feet.

If possible, seat the child at the end of the table away from others' elbows and feet. Seat the child next to the quietest, most tolerant sibling and avoid the child with whom the FASD child fights.

If the child is agitated or confused at meal time, you may need to keep routines the same at every meal. Consider having the same meals on the same days. This helps children with sequencing difficulties to 'know' the day of the week. You can try doing this for school lunches as well.

Serve the FASD child first, if they have trouble waiting for others to be served. You may want to try having the child do some of the serving. This lets them get up and do something physically active several times during the meal, and gives them an important role to play at meal time. Avoid putting any dessert on the table until after the child has eaten their first course.

If 'eating all night long' or late-night eating is a problem, establish rules about eating at the table only and allow one light snack just before bed.

Reduce distractions at mealtimes. Avoid having the TV or radio on and too much conversation. Save distracting socialising for after the meal, although this may be difficult as meals are often a key social time for families.

When eating out, avoid restaurants at peak times. Look for quiet places with low light and minimal noise, preferably where the child is known to the staff, where they understand the child and are tolerant of any behaviour problems.

Remember that any behaviour which is well-established during mealtimes at home will not necessarily transfer to other situations. Table manners will need to be taught at home, at school lunch time and then again in a restaurant.

9 Sleep – and the lack of it!

Children with FASD often have difficulties with transitional periods and activities where there is little or no structure. Bedtime contains elements of both, and can pose problems for children with FASD from a very early age.

Sleep, or the lack of it, is a big issue particularly in younger children. Patterns vary. The child either needs more sleep than other children or does not sleep at all. Sleep problems have a number of different causes. The affected children often lack an internal body clock and their melatonin levels (the hormone which leads to sleep) can be low. In addition, the children may have no concept of time. They struggle to differentiate between night and day and to understand that night time means sleep.

For all carers, it can be exhausting and challenging to care for a child who does not sleep engaging in a nightly battle to establish a regular sleeping routine.

Carers who are married or in a relationship can spend their evenings battling with the child rather than in conversation with each other, and then their bed is invaded by a little person in the middle of the night! Lack of sleep then impacts on everyone the next day. The tired child unable to cope in school, tired carers struggling at work and everyone is stressed, snappy and feel like the world is ending! The key is to establish a firm and calm routine as soon as possible.

Babies and toddlers

It is especially important to establish good sleep patterns as early as possible. For foster carers and other substitute carers there can be an added challenge as they may also have to undo previously learnt 'bad' routines. It can be particularly hard to establish routines in babies, who have spent long periods in hospital or had multiple placement moves.

For such children, you may find you have to sit with them and hold their hand, giving them additional security. Rocking the baby helps, wrapping them up in a soft blanket and holding them close, with their ear on your chest so they can hear your heartbeat. Parents have successfully used putting the baby in the car seat and driving round the estate in a continuous loop, a rocking chair, popping them in the pram or pushchair and pacing up and down the living room floor. A warm bath before bed may help the child fall asleep.

Older children

Firstly, decide what time you want the child in bed. Remember your child cannot tell the time. It is up to you to decide what time is bedtime. Then establish a clear bedtime routine. If it helps write it out on a whiteboard or pin a sheet to the fridge door clearly stating who does what and at what time!

Even if the child rebels or complains, it is important that you stick to the routine without fail every night, even in the school holidays. Only modify the routine if the child is unwell. Affected children also have poor immune systems and tend to have a lot of minor illness. Illness also interferes with sleep patterns, so you have to be firm, but also realistic. Do not change the routine on holiday or weekend visits to family and friends. Many parents have found that by sticking to the routine in the same order, they were able to get their child to settle to sleep, or at the very least in bed at the same time, wherever they travelled.

With older children, it is often easier to accept that they must remain in their bedroom after a certain time even if they are not asleep. Agreed activities in their room, for example a book or a CD with headphones so the rest of the household is not disturbed will help the child who needs little sleep to be less of a strain on the rest of the family.

For all children, the strategies which we have found helpful include:

1. A set routine. Establish a definite bedtime and stick to it, even during summer holidays and when the clocks change. Establish clear bedtime rituals for saying goodnight which visually allow a transition from the 'getting ready for bed' routine to the bed itself. Always encourage the child to sleep in their own bed.

2. Have a calming routine that starts an hour before bedtime. This sends a clear signal to the child that bedtime is approaching. For example, the child clears away their toys, has a warm bath, brushes their teeth, gets into their pyjamas, says goodnight to rest of the family and goes to their bedroom for a story. Do not let the child watch exciting videos or TV programmes or play computer games in this calming time. Discourage partners who arrive home late from work from playing boisterous games in this settling down period. Leave these activities until the weekend.

3. Try reading a story to younger children that ends with the animals or characters going to

bed and sleeping. A favourite soft, squidgy toy or blanket to cuddle may help. However only allow one toy or book in bed with them, the one they choose for that night.

4. Give a drink of warm milk or camomile tea. Lavender oil drops on their pillow or in their room help some children.

5. Ensure the child's nightwear is comfortable without scratchy labels, tight elastic, loose threads or sticking-in seams.

6. Ensure the bedroom is dark, quiet and free from clutter and visual distractions. If the child wishes, have one light in the room, by the bed and insist all lights are out except that light. Sometimes it can be little things, such as a red 'standby' light on an electrical item that disturbs your child. Keep the other furnishings in the child's bedroom to a minimum.

7. Ensure bedding is comfortable and securely tucked in. Some children are comforted by the weight of an extra blanket.

8. Reassure the child about where you will be and what you are going to do when they are in bed.

9. Give very explicit instructions and tell your child exactly what to do. 'Lie down now, in a cosy sleeping position, shut your eyes, no talking.' Use the same words each night, giving the next instruction once the first one has been complied with.

10. Avoid getting into the habit of having a cosy chat or a deep and meaningful conversation when your child is in bed. Try to do this downstairs before the bedtime routine starts. If you have other children and are reading to them all, maybe sit on your bed, have a story and a chat, then move into your child's bedroom for 'sleeping time'.

11. If your child is a chatterbox, then be very firm and clear: 'no talking, sleeping time, goodnight.'

12. If your child has a habit of popping out of bed, then scoop them up, take them back to bed and settle them in. Be very clear. 'Stay in bed, sleeping time, good night.' Or, 'This is your bed; this is where you are supposed to be'. Every time the child gets out of bed repeat the same identical words like a broken record!

13. You may have to accept the fact that your child is in bed but not asleep. For children who wake up at night, have a list of

acceptable things for the child to do in an acceptable place. For example the child can have the radio on very low with reasonable relaxing music if this helps relax them so they can go to sleep.

14. Safety-proof the house for night time wandering. Lock all doors. Place locks near the top of the doors so the child cannot reach the lock. Consider installing a single alarm system that lets you know when the child has passed a certain point. Before that point, let the child wander. Make sure that this area is entirely child-proofed. A gate across the bedroom door may be useful.

Remember, all children will eventually reach teenage years and many parents have found that it does get easier as the child gets older. If you are fortunate, they will eventually not want to get out of bed in the morning, except for Saturdays when you don't need to get up!

10 Crying, anger, aggression, temper tantrums and meltdowns

Children with FASD are over-sensitive and easily overwhelmed by their environment. They become distressed, throw a tantrum and then 'get stuck'. They are unable to stop the tantrum because they do not know what to do next and are poor at self-soothing. Aggressive behaviour is especially common in young boys and is often especially worse at home immediately after school. So, what is going on? How do we control or prevent such behaviour breakdowns and help our children handle their emotions?

Prevention is always the key. Frequently it is environmental factors and external things in the world around the child that triggers the meltdown. One of the reasons parenting these children is such hard work is the pre-planning and analysis that their parents have to do! They need to take time to step back, consider, reflect, think through and identify what 'triggers' their child's behaviour.

The most common reason for tantrums is because the child is tired and has sensory overload. Avoid situations where the child is over-stimulated by light, movement, sound, toys, noise, colour, activities or crowds. Avoid large shopping centres at peak times. The FASD child may find it very difficult to habituate to (screen out) background noise.

If a child has been sitting at a desk all day in school, we should not be surprised that they need to 'explode' when they come home. FASD children have an inbuilt need for movement. Many suffer from hyper-mobile joints and muscles. It is often easier for them to move their limbs than it is for them to struggle and force their muscles to keep still. Therefore, parents may have to accept that when the child comes out of school they are going to need half an hour of total unrestrained movement and madness!

Build that need into your daily life. Let the child run round a coffee table (not a glass-topped one) in circles. Put large beanbags and cushions on the floor and allow the child to fling themselves repeatedly onto the soft surface. If the weather is good, take them to the park and let them run wild. If you are concerned about their safety in a park get a trampoline and put it in the back garden. Ask your GP to refer you to a physiotherapist or occupational therapist. They can give you programmes to improve your child's muscle tone and to reduce their sensory overload.

Many children with FASD have meltdowns when faced with too many choices. To make a choice the child has to hold two concepts in their mind at the same time and compare them. This process is very difficult for the alcohol-affected child. For example, a 7-year-old girl had horrendous and inexplicable tantrums every morning. Once however her parents stopped asking her what she wanted to eat for breakfast and which cereal she wanted and what clothes she wanted to wear and simply gave her a breakfast cereal and handed her an outfit, the tantrums stopped. They then gradually re-introduced choice but in a very limited way. They put just two breakfast cereals boxes on the table so that she could visually look at the boxes and then choose. Are you facing your child with too many choices? If so limit the number of choices; your child simply cannot cope with them.

Use photographs of actual people, places, and important things to prepare a child for events such as moving to a new home, going to the dentist or doctor, going to the hospital or going to a new school. The unexpected or unexplained absence of a family member, even for a short holiday, can be very upsetting to the child. Use photographs of the person and the place where they are to explain their absence. If a child has to move to a new foster or adoptive home, or is even attending a sleep-over, try to keep the child's daily routines as normal as possible. Consistency and routine will minimise negative impact of the change. Acknowledge the child's fears about abandonment and other separation issues. Be as reassuring as you can while still being realistic. Help them work through separation issues in advance of any impending move.

Alcohol-affected children do not cope well with any transitions. They find it very difficult to end one activity and start another. They can get stuck into one activity and are unable or unwilling to move on. Asking them to stop what they are doing often causes a tantrum. For example, a 12-year-old girl loves the sensation of the hot water in the shower and dislikes getting out. When asked to, she will even write 'no' in the steam on the glass shower door. Her parents have to ask repeatedly and calmly for her to get out and 'bribe' her with the promise of another activity she enjoys, like shopping! They have now found it better to make it clear that she is going to get showered and dressed because the family is going out shopping.

Hard though it is, parents have to be patient or the situation will escalate out of control as they become more stressed, and no one will achieve anything! Give yourself time to complete basic daily tasks. Get up earlier in the morning and prepare as much as you can the night before. Rushing a child and making them hurry will result in stress for everyone and means everything takes twice as long.

Designate a calm, cosy, comfortable place for 'quiet time and space' in your home where the child can go when they feel they are becoming overwhelmed. This strategy will, over time, help your child to learn to self-regulate their out-of-control emotions. No matter how frustrated and angry you are, remember that shouting, losing your temper, arguing with a child or physically punishing them will always make the situation worse. Children need help with a situation they find bewildering. Adults losing control and becoming angry with them will always add to their fear and distress and their feeling that the situation is now totally beyond anyone's control.

Make it very clear that this 'quiet time' is not a punishment and the 'quiet space' is not a 'naughty corner'. An older child might like to be in their bedroom with the curtains closed or the lights dimmed with relaxing music playing. Younger children often prefer a pile of cushions or blankets in a room downstairs where they are closer to their parents. Some parents find a 'tent' made by putting a blanket over a table or settee helpful. If anger is a problem, have a safe place for the child to express it in some physical manner for example bouncing on a trampoline, kicking a ball or banging a beanbag.

Some very tolerant parents have even used frantic drumming successfully, but make sure you have very tolerant neighbours first! Being over-stimulated is very frightening for a child, so an adult should always be nearby and check on the child frequently until they calm down.

Whilst prevention is always the best choice, there will still be times when an eruption occurs and you will need to talk your child through and out of the tantrum. Get down on the floor, under the bed clothes, under the table or wherever they have retreated. Sit down or lie down with them. Speak in a clear, firm voice and say, 'You are cross/angry/sad/upset/scared'. Clearly name the emotion for them.

However, you must also have decided, before you get down with them, what you are going to do next. You will need a clear, predictable, individual routine which you know will soothe your child. Every parent knows their child's sensory issues and whether it is good to touch them, wrap them in a blanket, hold them close or sit them on their knee. Touch and close physical contact will make other children much worse.

Once you have calmed the child, move them onto a beanbag or large cushion and cuddle them. Finally distract them by moving them on to an activity which they enjoy and find soothing. Younger children like tactile activities such as sand or water play. Older children may prefer some time on a games console or watching a familiar soothing DVD or TV programme. Other well-tried soothing strategies include sitting quietly in a rocking chair or hammock; taking a warm bath or shower or listening to quiet music through headphones.

All FASD children struggle to name emotions and understand them. You will need to teach them the meaning of emotions like 'happy' and 'sad' from a very young age. Tell your child clearly and on a daily basis what emotion they are feeling. Tell them also when you or other family members are sad or happy. Many people say their FASD child lacks empathy, but this is not true. They can be very kind, caring, sensitive children who just struggle to correctly identify the right emotion in the right situation and need help and prompting.

Work with the teacher and other children to explain how your child feels things differently. The phrase, 'keep hands to yourself' is meaningless to the FASD child. Be specific and say 'keep your hands in your pockets' or 'put your hands on the desk'. These children can struggle with spatial awareness, so mark out the area they should sit or stay in with rugs, mats or masking tape. At home, give them their own marked chair in the living room and their own play corner. Ask the teacher to place your child at the beginning or end of a line, not in the middle.

Hyperactivity is a common problem for children with FASD. Parents can help control the problem by carefully structuring the child's activities and by reducing the amount of external stimulation. Avoid cluttered spaces inside and outside the home. Clutter increases hyperactivity. Limit TV-watching and avoid video games if this causes the child to become overstimulated.

Avoid letting a child concentrate for long periods of time. Concentration is hard work and very physically tiring. Alternate activities requiring concentration like studying or washing dishes with physical exercise such as running, tumbling, dancing or trampolining. Give your child lots of opportunities to be physically active. Sports such as soccer and gymnastics for older children are excellent ways to use up all that energy. These activities promote healthy self-esteem and may give a child who struggles in school a taste of success in another area of life. Group sports activities may help the child to make friends.

All children should learn to swim and swimming is also a very good physical outlet for many hyperactive children. The ability to swim could also be a lifesaver one day. Some children however become distressed by the noise, splashing, water movement and the distortion of sound which occurs a large swimming pool. For these children, group swimming lessons may be counter-productive.

Private lessons when the pool is empty may be preferable.

Remember that highly-charged social activities such as birthday parties, weddings and Christmas may simply be too overwhelming for a child with FASD. Limit the number of visitors to your home if this is overwhelming for the child.

Try to socialise with your friends when the child is asleep, not at home or at school. Many parents have found their child has a substantial increase in energy levels and more distracting behaviour when extra people are around, especially people the child does not know!

All parents however need a social life and some adult friendships. No one can be an effective parent 24/7. Time away from your child will help you to function as a better parent the next day and you will relax enjoy yourself more without the need for constant vigilance. So make sure you find opportunities to go out and enjoy yourself and do not feel guilty. Parents looking after themselves as well as their children is the key to survival.

11 Communication

Try this! Turn on all the televisions and radios in your home. Sit for three minutes and listen to all the information being presented to you. Then take a piece of paper and try to summarise all the verbal information you have been bombarded with. This is how a child with FASD perceives the world of spoken language and why they will struggle to make sense of language every day of their lives.

Children with FASD are often late to speak. Damaged and misaligned teeth with poorly formed or faulty enamel are common. Cleft lips and palates also occur more commonly in children with FASD. Sometimes surgery is required to repair cleft lips and palates; for others the subtle damage to teeth may interfere with their ability to make sounds correctly. Problems with coordinating fine motor skills can affect the ability of the child to use the muscles in the tongue, lips, teeth, throat and larynx which are necessary to make speech sounds. Other children appear to have no physical damage but still have delayed speech and language.

However, once the FASD child starts to talk, the children are described politely as 'chatty' and more commonly by their parents as children who 'could talk both hind legs off a donkey'. Unfortunately, this torrent of spoken language usually conceals a devastating inability to understand language. This difficulty with understanding and processing information which is given verbally is at the heart of the massive frustration felt by carers, teachers and others. How can this apparently bright, intelligent, chatty child not follow and obey a simple adult-led instruction?

Speech and language therapists distinguish between spoken language or expressive language and the understanding of language or receptive language. Normally this distinction does not matter because although a child's ability to understand language usually develops slightly before their ability to a speak it, the two are essentially developing together. Typically developing children normally start to speak around the age of 18–24 months. Before the child starts to speak however, most parents will tell you that the child 'understands everything that is said to them'.

Although most parents and teachers assume that understanding and spoken language are at the same level of development, this pattern does **not** occur in the FASD child. The classic speech and language development of the FASD child is very different. It is quite common to have a 5-year-old FASD child whose expressive language is at the level of a 7-year-old, but whose receptive understanding of language is that of a 2-year-old. We have seen many superficially articulate teenagers whose understanding of language is at the level of a 6-year-old. This gap is usually missed and is rarely properly assessed, but it has major consequences for the child and their family.

When a child genuinely does not understand what they are being asked to do, they simply cannot do it! This apparent refusal to obey instructions is not the behaviour of a child who **won't**, but of a child who **can't** do what is being asked of them. Unless the problem with understanding verbal instructions is recognised, there is a real risk that the child will become labelled as naughty, disobedient or even oppositional and defiant. The child is then shouted at, told off, punished or given consequences for their failure to obey. Punishment however only increases the child's sense of failure and makes them even more insecure and frightened.

In addition, even when the alcohol-affected child understands what is being asked of them, he or she will take longer to process the answer to a question. This is because to formulate a reply, the child will need to retrieve information from their memory. For example, 'What did you do at school today?' is a deceptively simple question but one which needs a memory of what has happened in the last six hours.

Finally, the child has to plan and organise themselves to comply with an instruction. They struggle with sequencing, remembering instructions and are very easily distracted. For example a parent may say, 'Go and put your clean clothes on your bed'. The child will go upstairs but, much to the carer's frustration, will be found half an hour later still in their bedroom, playing with something else. The carer's understandable frustration and impatience can sometimes have amusing consequences. One mother, tired of waiting for her daughter to reply to a question, fired a second question at her. Her daughter then replied to the first question, resulting in a slightly surreal conversation!

The child can also be accused of telling lies. The children who do this are often in the less severely affected group and are more defensive and aware of their deficits. Their faulty memories and inability to sequence sentences means they have a tendency to 'fill in the gaps' in order to answer a question.

Some children become quite adept at using this coping strategy and can tell very credible stories to compensate for their lack of understanding. They will frequently respond by talking about an incident they have seen on the television or use another memory of something that happened to them in the past. Unfortunately the child now adds untruthfulness to their increasing list of undesirable behaviours.

So, how do we communicate successfully with our children, help others to communicate with them and most importantly, help our children to communicate with us?

Do everything in your power to get your child assessed by a speech and language therapist. Their spoken speech may sound good, but when analysed is often found to be echoic or repetitive. All FASD children need a comprehensive assessment of their ability to understand language. The test we would recommend is called the CELF (The Clinical Evaluation of Language Fundamentals). It looks at core language, receptive language, expressive language, language structure, language content, language memory, and working memory. It takes about 45 minutes to complete and may be available locally on the NHS. It is however so important that we would recommend that if it is not available and you can afford it, pay for it and beg, borrow or steal if you can't! It is probably the only assessment that will make your child's behaviour and struggles in school understandable.

See a dentist regularly. Look after your child's teeth and make sure they (or you) clean them regularly. Parents may need to supervise dental hygiene for many years!

Thirdly adjust your expectations and encourage everyone else dealing with the child to be the same. Assume that, however superficially articulate your child seems to be, their understanding of language is probably about half their chronological age (or even less). You need to be patient. You must understand that even though your child seems to be deliberately disobeying you, they simply do not understand what you are asking them to do.

Change and simplify your own language. All parents, especially mothers, use too much language and too many unnecessary explanations when talking to their children. Teachers can be even worse offenders! For example take the very simple instruction, 'Before you go out to play in the garden put your coat and hat on.' That sentence however makes no sense if your child does not understand that little word 'before'. Your child will probably know that you are talking about his hat and coat but is not sure what you want him to do with them and when. You are also giving him the instructions in the wrong order in that supposedly simple sentence.

83

Try instead speaking like an old fashioned telegram where all the inessential words have been left out: 'Stephen' (using his name will to get his attention), 'hat on, coat on, then play in the garden'. Using simple language solves frequently more behaviour problems than expensive therapy and ineffective parenting classes!

Begin all conversations with the child's name and make eye contact with them. You must use their name and ensure you have their full attention before you speak. Your child's name is not 'Oi' or 'You'. In school, expressions which start with 'class' or 'group' will be ignored. Teachers should not be surprised when the child does not respond to instructions to 'the red table' or 'Mrs Smith's group'.

Think about what you are saying. Be very clear, be very concrete and say exactly what you want them to do. For example, 'tidy up' is too abstract. Instead say, 'Pick up the bricks and put them in this box'. Often with a request like this, particularly with younger children, you might need to follow this instruction up by showing them yourself what to do. If you do this, be even more specific and repeat the instruction again as you do it 'Pick up the bricks and put them in the box. I will pick up this one; you pick up that one.' Use the same words for daily routines. 'Brush your teeth' is better than 'Clean your teeth' or 'Get your teeth done'. 'Put your pyjamas on' is better than 'Get ready for bed now'. Break down tasks into small steps and teach each step through repetition.

Avoid negative instructions. Tell your child what you want them to do, not what you don't want them to do. For example, instead of shouting, 'Don't run', say instead, 'Walk, please'. Be very specific about what you want them to do. For example 'Sit on that chair and play with your Lego' is better than 'Stop messing about the kitchen'. 'Put your coat on the hook on the door' is much better than 'How many times have I told you not to leave your coat on the floor?'

Be brief and keep instructions short. The child may have a short attention span, even though they may appear to be listening. Multi-step directions should be given gradually and only if you are sure that your child has the ability to follow more complex directions. A series of sequential pictures may help. There is no definite time when this will occur and some children will need help with understanding verbal instructions throughout their lives.

Speak slowly and pause between sentences to allow for processing. Auditory processing may lag behind rate of speech. Repeat and repeat instructions. Expect to have to ask a child to do something 20 times before it finally 'sinks in' and they respond correctly. If they respond quicker, then that is great.

You may however have to give the same instruction 20 times again tomorrow. Constant unending repetition is often the main guarantee of success.

Many words or expressions have more than one meaning, and it is helpful to teach these different meanings. Children with FASD are often very literal in their understanding. When a teacher says 'How many times have I told you not to do that?' the child will miss the rhetorical nature of the question and produce a correct but socially unacceptable answer such as 'Three times today and twice yesterday Miss'. Rudeness and insolence is then added to the list of the child's many perceived failings!

When the child needs to focus on a task or listen to you; you may need to keep the environment as free from the distractions as possible. Avoid giving important instructions against a background of the television, radio, video games and other people talking. For some children, an FM transmitter/receiver (also known as a body pack hearing aid) has proved to be very useful for screening out distracting noise in school.

Lists for older children that also include step-by-step simple instructions on how to do the things on the list can be a useful life skill for both common and unexpected situations. Teach the child how to use a list and practice with role-play and simulation games. If the child does not know what to do next, jog their memory. Tell, demonstrate, show and then find a visual way to tap into their memory. Teach the child a visual or verbal cue to help them understand it is time to begin the task. If the child cannot remember, remind them again, take ten deep breaths and move on.

Transitions and moving from one activity to another can be difficult. Alcohol-affected children can even experience difficulty in the simple changes that occur every day, such as moving from one activity to another. This may even be the case when the child is being asked to change their focus from a less pleasant task to a more pleasant one. Try to measure time in a concrete and visual way as well as a verbal way. For example, you might end your instructions with the word 'now'. Egg timers are a useful way to clearly define the length of an activity which a child is reluctant to stop. Give the child advance warning that an activity will be over soon. For example 'This is the last game'.

Gentle reminders and cues help produce positive behaviours and reduce the child's sense of failure and embarrassment. Give the child simple verbal cues about new situations. For example, 'when we go to the hairdressers, we go in and sit down on a chair and wait until it is our turn. When the lady cuts your hair you can play your video game'. Afterwards praise the child for 'sitting still' not for being a 'good girl'! You will need to repeat this sequence every time you go and use the same salon! Link one task with another to help establish sequences, for example: dinner comes after homework; the school bus comes after breakfast; story time comes after the bath.

Use expressive gestures when talking. Try varying the loudness, inflection and tone, of your speech and use hand signals. Use as many visual cues as possible to trigger memory and to aid comprehension. Use exaggerated facial and body language to get the message across.

Be very specific when labelling inappropriate behaviour for example. 'John does not kick' can be combined with an exaggerated shaking of the head. Touch can be useful for teaching appropriate social distance from others. For example place your straight arm on the child's shoulder and say 'this is where we stand when we talk to our friends'. For children who invade the personal space of others, practising talking with a hula hoop around their waist helps to visually reinforce the idea keeping a fixed distance from others.

Help the child to interpret social and behavioural cues of others. For example 'That person looks happy because...' Help the child to express their emotions in acceptable ways. Encourage the use of positive feelings: 'I can do this!' 'I can work this out!'

Often children with language disabilities have difficulty with the 'why'-, 'what'-, and 'where'-type questions. Use alternative, more specific, concrete explanations instead. For example, do not say 'why was the boy's mummy cross?' It is better to ask 'Why did the boy knock the milk over?' and when you get an answer, add 'This made his mummy cross, because she had to wash the floor again'. Spend time discussing cause and effect relationships and why things happen. Be patient with your child's delayed ability to learn about the relationship between actions and consequences.

12 Praise, reward, consequences and discipline

A major issue for all who care for children with FASD is discipline: how to stop undesirable or dangerous behaviours and then helping the child find ways not to do it again! First, always remember that the child's frontal lobes have been damaged by the alcohol exposure. This is the part of the brain that controls behaviour and judgement. Processing deficits make it difficult for the child to connect actions with consequences and to feed back this learning to their behaviour. Secondly, the child with FASD can be as naughty as any other child! Always ask yourself if the child's misbehaviour is due to a lack of comprehension or wilful lack of compliance.

Over time, you will have to learn to distinguish wilful disobedience from the consequences of alcohol exposure on brain function. It is probably fair to say that the majority of the FASD child's undesirable behaviours are due to their faulty memory, social ineptness, lack of impulse control, the wrong influence of others and being completely overwhelmed by all the visual and other stimuli around them.

It is always better to pre-empt problems as discussed in previous chapters. Intervene before inappropriate behaviour escalates. Instead of trying to change the child, change the child's environment. This includes changing the child's physical surroundings, particularly minimising chaos and lack of structure and routine. Designate a place for 'quiet time' when the child feels overwhelmed. Just as important is changing the way other people interact with the child. When family members, teachers, and communities all understand the nature of FASD, they will change their expectations of the child and relate to him or her in a different way. As a result the child's behaviour will improve.

It is also important to remember that all those traditional techniques – sticker charts, tokens, time out and reward structures – do not work. Avoiding these techniques will save parents a lot of stress and a lot of frustration.

Always adjust your expectations before deciding on appropriate ways of behaviour management. The child will not be able to consistently function at age level. Divide the child's chronological age by two and assume that the child's ability to function will be around that level. A 4-year-old will act like a 2-year-old most of the time. A 10-year-old will act like a 5-year-old. A 16-year-old may act like a 4-year-old sometimes, like a 10-year-old sometimes and sometimes like an adult. The older the child is the better they will be at acting their age, but it is often just an act. The teenager's ability to function socially and emotionally is often around the 6-year-old level.

All children with FASD require close supervision and some need 24/7 supervision. A lack of impulse control and poor judgement means the decisions they make are not always wise and may put them at serious risk. Provide a level of supervision that allows them the maximum freedom without putting themselves or others at risk. This is a very tricky balancing act to get right. When in doubt, make your decision based on what is safest for the child. This can be a particularly difficult issue for foster carers, who are often overruled by social workers who do not understand FASD and think it is time for the child to have some independence in preparation for leaving care. Whether an FASD child can ever truly leave care and live as a completely independent adult is a major issue, which the British care system is not currently dealing with appropriately. Once freedoms are given to the child, it is very difficult to take them away later.

The wise parent will only let the child take very small steps toward independence only when they can demonstrate a long-term ability to handle time alone at home or in social situations. Do not take unnecessary chances and do not give in to pressure from others if it goes against your intuition. If you give the child too much freedom and something traumatic happens, the child will not learn from the incident and the guilt you will experience will very painful. Most parents whose older children ended up in serious trouble wish they could turn back the clock and provide closer supervision to their child from a very early age.

Always be positive rather than punitive. Remember that most of the time the child cannot control their behaviour. Even when actions seem deliberate or manipulative, this is really the nature of FASD. Be supportive and respectful. Remember that your role is not to watch for misbehaviour to punish, but to encourage safe, healthy, respectful behaviour and model that behaviour yourself.

Avoid all forms of physical punishment. The FASD child learns by imitating others and if others are physically aggressive with them, they will become physically aggressive with others. When physical aggression is learned at a young age, it is very difficult for the child to unlearn this behaviour later. There are ways to apply non-punitive means of discipline. They take time to learn and effort to apply, but it is worth it to prevent behaviours in the child that could lead to violence, abuse, injury or problems with the criminal justice system in the future

Imagine if you can't learn from the past and you are always in the moment. This means that everything is brand new every day. Therefore the golden rule is to deal with all behaviour whether it is negative or positive, instantly. This means that your reaction, positive or negative, is immediately associated to the behaviour at that time. Any delay in reaction means that the child forgets the incident and then cannot change any inappropriate behaviour or have their good behaviour reinforced.

Give instant praise and instant feedback. Give your child a hug and say 'well done' or 'thank you for walking into the room and sitting down quietly on the chair'. You can also use exaggerated facial expressions and body language to convey your pleasure by for example putting two thumbs up and having a big smile on your face. Be very specific with praise (and criticism), for example say 'Joey, good sitting' or 'Susie, good listening', and add a gentle touch on the child's head or arm. Simply saying 'good boy' or 'good girl' is meaningless to the child and will not help them to learn. There is no point in giving a longer-term reward, as the child will not relate their positive behaviour to the reward when it eventually arrives. Encourage the child to 'help' and make them feel a valued member of the family. Give the child positive acknowledgement and regard for just being themselves as well as for desirable behaviour.

If your child is engaged in an activity that is wrong, for example, kicking a wall or even another child, intervene promptly. Clearly say 'No! Stop! We do not kick'. The second golden rule is that you must also tell the child what you want them to do instead. For example, 'Do not kick the wall. Sit on the chair'. Again, use exaggerated facial expressions and body language to convey your displeasure. So say to the child, 'No, we do not kick walls' and put two thumbs down, frown and shake your head.

If you are not careful, you can spend all your time telling your child, 'don't do that', 'put that down', 'stop that'. You can begin to feel quite negative yourself. Hard though it might be, it is good to stop and rephrase your language into what you want the child to do. You are then speaking of positives not negatives all the time.

Always tell the child what to do, not just what **not** to do. Letting children know what to do gives them a direction to take the behaviour and focuses on the positives while defusing the negatives. For example, 'Chris, put your feet on the floor, not on the table'.

When you have children consistently engaging in behaviour you do not want, for example, running into a room and leaping onto the furniture, decide what you want them to instead and then practise it. So in this situation take them out of the room immediately. Then, holding their hand, walk back into the room and sit down with them properly on a chair. Practise this several times. The next time they enter that room, stop them and ask, 'When you go in the room, where do you sit?' Eventually after repetition of showing them what to do, they will gradually learn what is expected of them in a given situation. The learning process will however be very gradual. A lot of repetition will be needed before the child finally understands what is expected of them. You may need to teach the behaviour again in a different situation, for example, when you visit a relative's home.

Never ask your child why they did something as usually the answer will be a very truthful but unhelpful one of 'I don't know'. You could try asking more specific questions such as 'when' or 'where' or 'who said' but do not be surprised if the child's faulty memory causes them to be unable to recall. Also, do not be surprised if several days later they suddenly remember and inform you of all the details!

Use consequences with care and don't expect them to work effectively every time. Consequences must be concrete and simple and must be applied immediately and consistently. Even then, the child may not learn, or may forget or make the same mistake again. Adapt the consequences to the child's functional age rather than actual age. Recognise your child's unique strengths and weaknesses, build on their abilities and interests and set realistic goals for performance.

Keep your house rules simple. Base them on what you want your child to do. The best house rule is 'Walk in the house' and not 'Don't run in the house'. It is important that you keep to your rules and do not bend them or relax them 'just this once'. Children with FASD do not understand this concept. Be firm. Set clear, consistent limits. Don't debate or argue over rules. Post family rules in simple words and/or with pictures. Separate the child from the behaviour. The action may be 'bad', but the child must never feel that they are a 'bad' person.

Do not negotiate, explain, or get into a debate – just enforce. Never make threats that you cannot carry out. These children will take you literally, and in addition the child learns that there are really no consequences because the threat is not carried out. For example, to stop a child jumping on the living room furniture, the family rule was 'Bottom on chair, feet on floor, or you sit on the rug'. The instant consequence was that when he leapt onto the furniture he had to sit on the rug not on the sofa with everyone else. This was applied instantly, without any argument: 'Sit on the rug now'.

The other issue to consider in terms of any sanction is your own sanity! The request to 'sit on the rug' was more about the fact that bouncing around on the sofa when everyone else was trying to watch TV was highly irritating to the whole family.

Consider also the safety of the child and other children. When removing a child from a situation to diffuse and calm down, once again separate the child (not a bad child) from the inappropriate behaviour. Say for example 'Your behaviour tells me you need a quiet time'. Always talk to a child when they are calm and reinforce that they are a good person. For example, some people have the rule 'If you hit, you sit'. So any child hitting another child is instantly removed and sent to sit on a chair separate from, but in the same room as, everyone else. Putting the child in a room by themselves is likely to cause even more problems. FASD children always need supervision.

Distraction or redirecting is also a good method to employ. If a child is about to engage in something that is wrong or dangerous, or you see that they are doing something that could lead onto something inappropriate, intervene and move them on to another activity, put a TV programme on or point out of the window at something interesting!

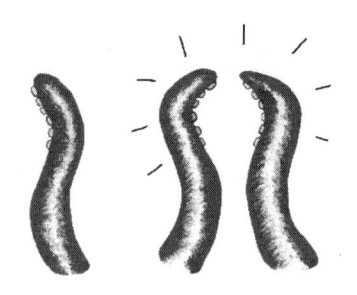

13 Arrested social development and the problems it causes

For many caregivers exposing their children to the wider world is where their major battles occur and is the source of their greatest fears. Scientific research has shown that children with FASD have an arrested social development that stops at about the level of a 4- to 6-year-old. It is therefore unreasonable for us to expect them to develop the social and moral conscience of an adult, or even that which we would expect of a typical 8-, 10-, or 12-year-old. The Americans rightly call the confused, often illogical thinking of the FASD child around moral and social issues 'innocent delinquency'.

Ownership and stealing

Ownership is a difficult concept to understand and it is particular difficult for the FASD child. FASD children have no concept of ownership, so will often take items that do not belong to them. They may not connect the object with the owner of that object. For example, they see a supermarket or shop packed full of interesting items which they want to pick up and play with and large stores often employ few people on the shop floor. Simply saying 'that's not yours' will not seem very logical to your child! The object is just sitting there, there is no one near it and it is not clear who it belongs to and to them it must therefore be free for the taking. They can slip into this mode of thinking even when they have repeated the rules about not taking things to you on many occasions. It is easier to teach your child what belongs to them than what is not theirs. Ensure that they understand that in shops if you want something you have to take it to the cashier and purchase it.

Having the possibility of your child being accused of stealing can be a major worry for the parents of older children. This is a situation where it is good to have the understanding of a wider community. Being surrounded by adults who have insight into your child's difficulties around ownership, who understand your child's poor impulse control and appreciate the fact that they cannot help picking up items is a major support for families. Understanding adults will also be more forgiving and less likely to go down a punitive legal route.

Be alert for new items in your child's possession. Ask them where they got it and if possible, simply return it. It is better to try to teach a child from the start what belongs to them using very clear unambiguous language. When a child picks up items in shops, ask 'Is that yours? No? Then put it back please'. You may have to 'frisk' them before they leave certain places or get into the habit of making them empty out their pockets. Always let them see you returning all the items they have picked up. Alternatively, ensure your child goes shopping in your company or that of another trusted individual.

Be alert as well for your child giving away their belongings. Ensure all items going into school or other places are clearly labelled with their name. We would recommend not letting them take valuable items such as mobile phones or games consoles into school or other groups where there is a possibility that your child will give it away, generously sharing with others.

Truth and lies

Making up stories and telling tall tales is a normal part of being a typical 4- to 5-year-old and many FASD children may not progress beyond this level of social development. It however is important for parents to try to distinguish between confabulations and lies, which are quite different things.

FASD-affected children **confabulate,** that is they spontaneously report events that never happened from time to time. These stories can be very convoluted and convincing! The inability to separate fantasy from reality is a common occurrence among people suffering from differing forms of brain damage. It is not a deliberate attempt to deceive. Confabulation in someone with FASD is caused by damage to the prefrontal cortex (frontal lobes) of the brain. This damage causes the individual to create and then to believe in false memories or perceptions. Sometimes the events did not happen at all and are based only in the imagination. At other times, FASD confabulations are caused by actual events that are combined with stories the child might have heard from others being all mixed together into a false memory or belief.

In addition, the FASD child will always struggle to differentiate between their thoughts and external events. They can honestly believe that they completed something just because they **thought** about it. They just didn't take the next step and turn that thought into action. Parents can interpret this as lying, unless they realise what is going on.

Being angry with or punishing a child who leads a parent or teacher on a wild goose chase caused by a confabulated memory is not uncommon. Always deal with your own feelings of betrayal, anger and fear for future before talking to the child. The fact is the child cannot be cured of this behaviour. He or she is not aware they are doing it. It is part of the executive functioning disorder of FASD and not a character defect.

It is always more appropriate to say, 'It sounds like you thought about it, but forgot to do it' rather than accusing a child of lying. This approach is less inflammatory than the accusatory statement 'You are lying to me'. Accusations do not get a parent any closer to having accurate information about what happened, which is often what they really want.

Lies are untruths told deliberately. Lies are usually much simpler than confabulations, and once you understand confabulation you should be able to tell the difference. For instance, if you see your child break a cup, hide the evidence and then tell you that they didn't do it, you have just been lied to. This is just human nature and usually done in order to get out of trouble and to the child may seem like a brilliant idea at the time.

Unlike confabulations, lies usually should be disciplined in some form. Your child needs to learn that it is not acceptable behaviour and that you expect him to learn to stop. You should do this even though lying and bad decision-making are often caused by impaired executive functioning skills, which is a characteristic of the brain damage caused by FASD.

Prevention is always better than cure. Supervision and routine are once again the key to success. The more parents can control the environment and the child's ability to act up in it, the less frequently the child will have the need to lie or even the opportunity to lie – and the parent will have to discipline the child less frequently about it.

Always use language that minimises the child having to tell you things from memory. This also decreases the possibility that inaccurate information will be given. For example 'Show me your homework' or 'Show me your nice clean room' is much better than 'Have you done your homework or have you cleaned your room?' Although this approach requires an inordinate amount of supervision it works because it will help the child to distinguish between thoughts and actions.

Tell your child that their brain works in a different way to other children. Help the child to ask themselves a list of questions and also help them to answer them. For example: 'Who can help me remember what happened at school?' or 'How do I know that I have done this?' These questions will be answered by things outside the child's own brain. Verify what happened in school with a classmate and teacher, or take the child up to the bathroom to see if she has actually used the soap and toothpaste.

Use non-verbal means of communication wherever possible. Always ask the school to write down all messages home or email them to you. Do not rely on your child's ability to recall and repeat verbal information. They are hopeless at it and will then make something up! This is not ill-intentioned and is usually just the opposite. Your child is trying hard to do the right thing but people around them are talking too fast, they can only process a few parts of a conversation or instructions and often don't even know they have missed large chunks of information.

If your child with FASD alleges that someone has hurt them or stolen from them, it is easy to discount their story. This happens especially if he or she has a history of taking the belongings of others without permission or of getting into fights at school with other children.

Before assuming that your child's story is either true or a confabulation, however, ask him or her enough simple questions to see if the story makes sense. There may be parts of the story that seem believable and other parts that cause the narrative to completely fall apart. Aim to get a consistent narrative even if that takes time and get as much as you can corroborated by others before taking any further action.

Personal hygiene

Many children with FASD are delayed in terms of developing age-appropriate toileting and hygiene skills. There are four main reasons for this. First, they have a damaged central nervous system which is functioning at a much younger age than their actual age. Secondly, they have problems with their fine motor skills and can struggle with tasks such combing hair or fastening buttons. Thirdly, they can have a medical problem which needs treatment (constipation is especially common). Finally, they have a poor short-term memory so they struggle to retrieve the information they need to carry out day-to-day tasks, such as getting dressed, showering, remembering to change a sanitary pad. Also, as any parent will tell you these children have no concept of time particularly first thing in the morning when there is a deadline to meet!

Many carers of children with FASD find toileting difficulties incredibly stressful, especially when children are starting school still wearing pull-ups or nappies and the school are unhelpful in their response.

It is important that you seek medical advice to ensure that any underlying medical condition of the bowel or bladder is identified and treated; such problems are very common in FASD affected individuals. Help can also be sought from the

Incontinence Nurse or Health Visitor; often they have suggestions or strategies to try which can be useful.

Secondly, difficult though it may be – especially in the middle of the night - try not to react to "accidents" with anger, irritation or any other negative emotion; instead respond in a calm and matter-of-fact manner and simply get the child to assist in cleaning up and changing. Over time, a calm and consistent response should achieve success, but do not be surprised if even in the teenage years occasional "accidents" occur, especially if the young person is ill or over-tired.

Not all hygiene strategies will work for all people with FASD. It will take trial and error to determine what works for each family. What is always critical is routine, repetition, organisational structure, and a willingness to try new strategies. Parents have found the following strategies helpful.

Children with FASD characteristically do not choose appropriate clothing for the weather. They struggle to understand concepts like 'summer' or 'winter' clothes and often choose bizarre clothing combinations which can make them a target for teasing by other children. Hang coordinated outfits together on combination hangers. Put pictures to indicate the weather, for example sun, rain or snow, on the appropriate clothes. Devise an organisational technique for hanging and storing clothing. Place picture codes on dresser drawers, or use under-bed storage drawers or coloured boxes for keeping items together

Encourage your child to monitor the condition of their clothing. Show them how you check for spills, stains or tears on your clothes. Teach your child to notice their clothing wear and tear. If a spill occurs, teach the child how to remove to it with spotting solution or dabbing with water. Role-model how you should sort laundry and how to use the washer and dryer. Let them do it themselves under supervision and praise them for getting it right.

It is essential to establish a daily routine of bathing or showering from an early age. By establishing a routine, the child does not have to remember when the last hair wash occurred or decide if a bath is needed. Maintain this routine even at weekends during school holidays and trips to family and friends.

- Keep supplies like shampoo, body wash, combs, and toothpaste in a single storage container. Always put the container in the same place in the bathroom.

- Let the child help to choose and buy their own toiletries in a colour which they like. Give them their own towel in a specific pattern or colour. This increases the enjoyment of using their own personal items.

- Colour-code and or label items such as towels, toothbrush, comb, and the child's personal storage container for quick identification.

- If long showers are a problem, put a timer in the shower that shuts it off.

- If overfilling the bath is a problem, use indelible ink to draw a line on the bathtub to prevent the child from overfilling the bath.

- Keep the hot-water tank temperature down or invest in a thermostat-controlled tap. This is essential for children who do not have a normal sense of pain and temperature and could easily burn themselves accidentally.

- Keep a daily task checklist. It can be in the form of a chart or picture-stickers or whatever works best for the child. The checklist can combine pictures and words and include the specific time for each task.

- When the child is old enough, begin teaching them to comb and style their own hair. Use other family members to model this and get them to talk about how important and enjoyable this can be.

- Post a homemade STOP sign on the bathroom door that lists the crucial items that must be done before leaving the room. Establish with the child a routine of checking the list (flush the toilet, turn off the water, get dressed, etc.).

- In school, ask the teachers to include activities related to hygiene on your child's daily plan, such as learning to check their hair and face in the mirror when in the bathroom and washing hands after each visit.

Puberty

Puberty marks a new stage of life in the life of any child. Children with FASD reach puberty at about the same time as their peers but their developmental delay and behavioural disabilities can cause different complications. Puberty has to be explained to your child at the level of their understanding. One girl heard about hormones and came to the conclusion that her feeling sad was due to her hormones 'falling over in my body'. Information should only be given as needed and when the child is ready. For example, many people mistakenly believe that teaching about periods has to include information about sex, but information about the monthly cycle can simply be given in the context of an explanation that this is your body getting ready for when you grow up and might choose to have a baby.

It is helpful to:

- Begin the routine of using deodorant at an early age, before the onset of puberty. This routine should be established early because by the time the child needs it, they will have become used to it.

- Model shaving with an electric razor, long before it is time for the boy with FASD to shave. When it is time to learn to shave, pick an electric razor that best suits the individual, and encourage the use of pre-shave lotion. As with bathing, encourage daily shaving to establish a set routine.

- Talk to your child about body changes in a simple way, incorporating discussions into everyday life. When puberty approaches, talk about the changes before they occur. If you see signs of very early puberty, seek information and medical advice.

- Get materials on puberty for young people with learning difficulties, even if your child has an average IQ. These materials use simple explanations and illustrations that are helpful for children with FASD who have difficulty understanding abstract concepts.

- Fathers, uncles, or older brothers (or mothers, if they are comfortable) should discuss nocturnal emissions ('wet dreams') and other normal characteristics of puberty in boys whenever they begin.

- Mothers or sisters may be able to talk about their own menstruation cycle and care in a natural way before the daughter's cycle begins.

- Establish a schedule for changing sanitary pads if remembering is a problem. Maintain this schedule whether or not a change is needed. In school, it is helpful to have a named adult to ensure your child's sanitary pad is changed or, for older children, a trusted classmate.

Modesty is often an issue for families. Behaviour which is acceptable or even attractive in a young child is not acceptable in a young man or woman approaching puberty. People with FASD often become engrossed in what they are doing and do not think about consequences of their actions. They can be unaware for example of the social consequences of other people and children seeing them without clothes or of talking about periods in a public place.

From an early age, make it a family routine that after showering or bathing, everyone in the family always get dressed in the bathroom. Alternatively, when not taking a shower or bath, all family members should put on a dressing gown and get dressed in their bedrooms. Allowing a child to wander round the house semi-clothed and get dressed in front of the television might be acceptable at the age of 5 but is not at 15.

Although the typical developing teenager will disappear for hours behind locked bathroom or bedroom doors the instant any signs of pubertal change occur, entrenched habits in the FASD child can be impossible to change. They will simply not understand the reasons why different rules are now in place. Though it is difficult to instil a sense of modesty, parents must teach the skills that will protect their child from ridicule or even exploitation. Develop a concise easy-to-understand explanation of modesty and discuss it as needed, starting with every shower or bath. You will need it less often over time.

14 Friendships, social life and recreation

Friendships make for a richer, fuller life. Friends teach us important lessons and support us through troubled times. For the parents we meet, however, making long-term friendships is one of the greatest challenges for children with FASD.

This challenge comes from a number of different sources. The learning difficulties and possible lower IQ associated with your child's condition means that he or she might not understand social etiquette or the subtle ways of friendship. They may also struggle to understand the concept of 'personal space'. When meeting other children, they can stand too close to them, making them feel uncomfortable or irritated. Children with FASD are often less socially mature than other children of the same age and it can be hard for them to relate to their classmates as equals. Their inability to read social situations can make it easy for others take advantage of them and can make them targets for teasing or bullying. One parent commented:

'My child is incredibly innocent compared to other children her age. She's just not worldly or

sophisticated in social interactions. She copes well with friends but I don't think she understands the nuances of it all.'

Discouraging as this may sound, the good news is that – with structure and supervision – your child can enjoy positive social interaction. It will be challenging to achieve, and it will require lots of involvement from parents, but the rewards are plentiful. In fact, one parent told us that the more success her child found in friendship, the more success she had in her life. Unlike the typical child who can make and keep friendships without the direct involvement of a parent, most of the strategies used in FASD children require lots of parental involvement.

Supervise! Supervise! Supervise!

As well as information, supervision is always the key to success, even for older children. One common mistake is the widely held assumption that as the child is now 14 or 15, he or she needs to be independent. We have had many disastrous situations occur when parents or carers, pressured by society's perception that all young people need to be given freedom in order to be independent, have allowed children out without adequate supervision. Follow your own instincts as to what feels right for your child.

Build your own social safety net

As has been repeatedly stressed throughout this book, children who are affected by FASD need to be surrounded by a community who understands them and their needs. Sharing the diagnosis with friends, family and neighbours is a good starting point for ensuring your child gets the support they need. Parents find the involvement of the wider community gives them more opportunities for breaks and the young person more independence.

You will need to choose your own friends and your child's friends carefully. You will frequently find yourself having to explain to others the reasons for your child's rather odd behaviour and strange choices. Over time however, a cohort of friends who understand and accept your child will be slowly built up. Your friends must understand FASD in order to supervise and engage with your child. They must also know about the importance of modelling with them how to play and interact socially.

You also need to become creative as your child grows up. Give the child supervised independence within this group of friends who can act as surrogate carers. This is obviously easier to achieve in a small community. One mother who lives in a rural community is able to give her child complete freedom to explore the local annual village fete because every adult there has known her child for many years. She knows that everyone is keeping a discreet watch on her child and will quickly intervene if she has a problem.

> *We have found that our church has been a great resource as far as helping our son to make friends his own age. The children there belong to friends of ours and are prompted by their parents to be tolerant of his difference. This has helped him to gain some confidence and be able to make some friends in other situations.*

Make sure that your child's social time is always supervised either by you or by another caregiver who understands FASD. If your child goes to a friend's house to play, educate the other parents about FASD, and make sure they understand your child's needs. Teach them how they can help the children have a positive playtime experience. You could share with them some of the information sheets included in this book.

In school, supervision is particularly important at playtime, during the lunch break and before and after lessons. Speak to your child's teacher and see if you can set up a buddy system, which will ensure that no one particular child is over-burdened. It is best if a small group of children can have a rota and take it in turns to offer friendship in school. This will give your child positive social and play interactions and will keep them away from the naughty or disruptive children in the class (whom we can guarantee they will instinctively seek out).

> *'We had a young woman, about three years older than our daughter, spend about ten hours per week with her. It was important that our daughter perceived her as a friend who was 'cool', so hanging out was 'cool'. This was a major turning point, although it was not always a smooth road.'*

Join a local support group for families with children affected by FASD; The FASD Trust can help you find your nearest group. Involve your child's family and friends and support workers and encourage the friendships your child develops at these meetings. Meeting other affected children at a support group has been a very positive experience for most of the children we know.

Give your child helpful reminders and cues

Watch your child closely when she enters a new social situation and help her behave appropriately. For example, if he hugs someone he has just met, quietly remind him that hugging is for close friends and family members only. Suggest an alternative to hugging, such as shaking hands. Make lists or use pictures to explain which people the child can hug.

Before going into a new situation, teach your child, talking through beforehand what to do and how to behave. Give quiet verbal cues as you walk in to the room to remind the child of the right behaviour. Reminders will need to be given constantly until the child settles. Remember to reward good behaviour instantly.

Role play

Role-playing is a very effective tool in helping your child to understand how to act in social situations. Demonstrate appropriate behaviours, such as how to share, how to disagree or how to meet new people. Your child can then draw on these experiences in real life situations. Develop social stories. Create stories and scripts with pictures that describe common social activities such as waiting your turn or sharing. Suggest this tool to other people in your child's life.

Speech and language therapists can help with teaching social and conversational skills. Speak to your local therapy team and see if they run a summer course for teenagers focussing on social communication skills. They can often recommend other resources as well and give input to class teachers and carers.

Involve your child in group activities

Children with FASD often do well in activities or groups that are structured, such as Scouts, cadets or Brownies. They also enjoy and often are good at horse-riding, swimming, music, singing, gardening and art. This is an ideal way for them to make friends while having fun and participating in society. They also expose your child to organised social settings. Group activities can in addition meet their need to practice movement, coordination, balance and integrating sensory input. What starts as a hobby as a child could become the way the child earns their living as an adult.

Some children have difficulty in large groups, so monitor your child closely at the beginning or enrol them in a small group programme especially one tailored for children with special needs. You could also try one-to-one tuition initially before moving onto a group.

However, one word of caution, do not involve the child in too many activities. As these children are often hyper-active and "full of energy" some people try and engage them in constant activities, leaving no down-time, or space to chill out at home. This leads to these children being totally overwhelmed, exhausted and then to big emotional meltdowns. Instead try and choose just a couple of activities, carefully tailored to meet their needs, giving them a physical outlet and opportunity to socialise.

Always adjust your expectations about friendships in any groups. Try to avoid the two extremes of either expecting your child to have completely normal peer friendships or passively accepting that they will be socially excluded and isolated. Children with FASD often seek out younger or much older friends. Younger friends are usually chosen because their play skills and interests are at the same age as the FASD child. Older friends tend to be more tolerant of the FASD child and will often let them dictate the rules of shared play.

It's normal and healthy for your child to develop relationships with the opposite sex but it is important to keep them within safe boundaries. Educate your child about sex. Make sure your teenager knows the accurate words for all body parts and what it is acceptable to talk about in public. Provide constant reminders about the importance of privacy and modesty.

Know what is going on in your child's life, no matter how old they are

One issue which troubles many carers is the FASD child's ability to declare that everyone is their 'best friend'. They also have a tendency to home in on one person and demand their undivided attention.

We know of a 12-year-old girl, given her first mobile phone, who sent 80 text messages in one night to a classmate; a 13-year-old boy spending three hours sending Blackberry instant messages, another child hugging everyone in the supermarket queue innocently demanding, 'Do you love me?'. It is very important that these behaviours in fostered or adopted children are not labelled as attachment issues. It is nearly always due to a child's lack of understanding of socially appropriate behaviour.

While it is important to respect your child's privacy, it's equally important to understand what is happening in their lives. Supervise any television, computer or Internet activity and make sure you know whom they talk to on the telephone. These children are vulnerable and in particular could easily be caught up in chat room forums by those seeking to prey on the innocent and gullible. FASD children also quickly take on board and copy what they have seen in a TV programme. So avoid violence or other images that you do not wish your child to imitate. When it comes to TV, movies or computer games, remember that your child can't always understand the difference between reality and fantasy.

However, in terms of friendships and ability to relate to their peers, parents have to play a difficult balancing act. You will find, especially as they get older, that these children have a tendency to watch programmes for much younger children. It is therefore important for you to encourage and allow your child to view some age-appropriate programmes so that they can join in conversations at school with children. For example if every child in the class has watched *The X Factor* or the FA Cup Final on Saturday, the child who has not seen these programmes will be totally excluded from the playground conversation on Monday morning.

Own the diagnosis

As we have already mentioned, Professor Ann Streissguth's research in the USA (and our own experience here in the UK) demonstrates a clear link between positive outcomes as an adult for those who not only have a clear diagnosis but one which the child understands. When a child and family owns the disability and is clearly able to articulate it, the outcomes for them as adults are far more positive.

Many parents struggle to know when and how to share with their child the fact that they have FASD. Birth parents can be frightened of the child's response to them. Others become concerned the child will be labelled and stigmatised by others. However, research and our own experiences clearly indicate that honesty is always the best policy. The earlier the child knows, the longer they have to reach an understanding of their condition. More crucially, they will have time to accept that they have limitations and that there are tasks which they will always need help to complete, and it enables the child to learn how and who to ask for help.

The FASD Trust has produced a number of resources for children and young people about being affected by FASD. These materials are for their caregivers to share with them and have been designed to match the FASD child's more limited understanding. They can also be shared with their siblings and their friends in helping to explain what FASD is and how it has affected them.

Unsurprisingly, another of Prof Streissguth's key findings is that children who are in the same placement or family for as long as possible do better, because it gives a long timeframe for strategies and support networks to be built up. Children who frequently move placement have the worst outcomes of all. Stability between the ages of 8 and 12 seems to be particularly important.

15 The major problems of time, money and mathematics

These are areas in which all children and adults affected by FASD will struggle. For some their problems in these areas will be lifelong. This is because they are all abstract concepts which really hard to understand for people with FASD as the part of the brain that deals with these concepts is particularly affected by pre-natal alcohol exposure. In these areas you will often have to be your child's 'external brain'. They need your help to understand what they need to do and when they need to do it, and you may need to do it for them all their lives.

Time

Understanding time is hard. There is telling of time on a watch or a clock, the passage of time, such as 'dinner will be ready in 10 minutes', and there is also being on time, being early or being late. People with FASD learn best when they can touch and see objects and time cannot neither be touched nor seen.

A child with FASD has no internal clock. The passing of time, whether it is ten minutes or one hour, both feel the same. The child looks at the clock on the microwave and it says 8.00. He does not know if it means 8.00 in the morning or 8.00 in the evening. This is why affected children need so much adult help to keep their days organised.

People are also very inconsistent in how they express the time. People without the brain damage affecting people with FASD understand that 12.45 can be expressed as 'fifteen minutes to one' or 'a quarter to one' or 'twelve forty-five'. Most children will eventually learn that all these phrases mean the same time, but a child with FASD will think you are giving him three different times. You always need to be very consistent with how you express the time of day to your child.

The following strategies may help your child to understand time.

1. A digital clock is much easier for a child to understand than a clock with hands. Establish daily routines that will develop a structure to the day. Link the time of day to an activity such as 8.00am is time to brush teeth after breakfast or 7.00pm is time to

wash dishes or load the dishwasher after dinner. This will help the child develop good lifelong habits and this structure can largely replace the missing inner clock if it is done consistently.

2. Use a visual way to show that time is passing. An egg timer is useful for activities like showering and brushing teeth which may otherwise go on for a very long time! Buy an electric toothbrush which stops after two minutes if your child finds it hard to not know when to stop doing something.

3. Use an electronic timer with alarms to prompt the child. For example when is time to stop playing and get ready for bed. Teach your child how to set the timers themselves.

4. FASD always causes faulty memory. Teach your child to write down appointments and events in a diary and to refer to it often during the day. Mobile phones often can have a reminder or calendar system in-built that will give a young adult a daily prompt. This is where the early years of establishing a circle of friends and professionals around your child comes into its own. These adults will know they may have to remind the child to look at their programme and can also programme an entry into the young person's

calendar. Use texts as reminders for the more able child.

5. Write down what time the child has to leave for school in the morning. Tape this paper under the digital clock. Tell your child 'When the numbers match, it's time to go to school'.

6. Compare the passing of time to something the child might understand. For example, 'We will be at Granny's house in the time it takes to watch a *Fireman Sam* cartoon'.

7. Use the radio or TV to help the child understand when it's time to do something. For example, say 'It's time to go when this programme is over' or 'We will tidy up your room while we listen to one more song'.

Money

Problems managing money can lead to poor health, isolation, and dangerous situations for adults with FASD. Money can be a very abstract concept. You can touch money and hold it in your hand but what money can buy or what money can do are abstract ideas. The value of money is another concept which is also hard to understand. How much is something really worth? £50 for a bar of chocolate and £50 for a pair of shoes may both seem like good prices to the young adult with FASD. Cause and effect are also involved in managing money: an area which is fraught with difficulties for FASD adults. What is the connection between not paying your phone bill and your phone being cut off several weeks later? Why do people save money? How do you get out of debt?

Financial skills are hard to teach and will depend upon your child's level of understanding and academic ability. Be prepared for the fact that you will probably always need to have some degree of supervision or control over their financial affairs.

Utilise modern banking technology. Bills can be paid by direct debit, bank balances can be sent automatically by text to a mobile phone. There are a plethora of modern aids to money management that can be used. You might feel the need to be a co-signatory on bank accounts and able to assist directly with financial affairs.

If you are concerned about the longer-term after you have died, then get legal and financial advice and consider setting up something like a trust with named trustees or appointing a guardian. Many people think such things are only for the very wealthy, but they are not expensive or complicated to set up and in the long run could be a way of providing significant protection and support for your child.

It is better if the trustee is not a family member or friend. A trustee can help to manage money before it becomes a problem. The trustee will give the adult with FASD small amounts of money and supervise bill paying. There are also agencies that act as trustees. Ask your local community organisations for ideas or ask for a referral to organisations that provide this service. You can also look under 'lawyers' in the phone book for this service.

If your teenager is having trouble spending money wisely, you can help them out in many ways. Do not lend money and if you do, do not expect to get it back. Instead you can buy food, or gift certificates for a food store, a bus pass, gift certificates for haircut or local entertainment services like cinemas. **Never give the cash**.

Do not give expensive gifts. These are often sold for very small amounts of cash to more unscrupulous children and never bought back. **Avoid debit cards** and personal cheques. It is harder to spend money if the young person has to go to the bank when it is open. If a debit card it used, set up a daily withdrawal limit with the bank. Make a family rule that credit cards are not a good choice and make sure that your child does not have one.

Teach your teenager to use a notebook to write down which bills need to be paid and when they need to be paid. This will become their budget book. **Teach the child that bills are always paid first**. Write down everything else that they spend their money on like food, entertainment, clothes, and travel. Teach them to staple an envelope to the back of the book and keep all receipts. Help them to keep track of where they are spending money by going through these receipts with them regularly. **Teach them to keep their budget book in the same place all the time**. Have a trusted family member, friend or support person check that the bills are being paid and who can help with purchasing bigger items.

Big phone bills are a common problem. Set up account restrictions with the phone company. This could including no long distance calls and no additional features that you are charged extra for such as call waiting etc. Avoid paying for expensive roaming internet charges. Consider having an unlimited internet access contract or only allow the child to use Wi-Fi when it is free. If you let your child use the internet always carefully monitor what information your teenager is accessing.

16   Education matters

The whole issue of education and the child with FASD is sufficient subject to be a whole book in itself. The main focus of this book is parenting a child with FASD and life at home, but as education dominates a significant portion of a child's and therefore a parent's life, we just briefly here want to mention a few additional key points not made elsewhere in this book.

Not all children with FASD have significant learning difficulties; many have an IQ (intelligence level) in the low-normal range, but their other social functioning impairments impact on their ability to learn, as described previously in this book. Unfortunately, local authority assessments are often based on IQ and many parents describe their children as "falling between the cracks", as educationally they apparently are able, but emotionally and socially they struggle to fit with their peers. Many parents feel they are in a constant "battle" around school and education issues for their child.

There is no unique one-size fits all solution for education and the child affected by FASD. Some parents opt to home-school, some children need a special educational needs school, some children cope in mainstream with varying degrees of additional support. Other children attend specialist residential schools, sometimes paid for by their local authority. Some parents pay for their children to be educated privately.

In addition to parental choice, preference and financial means, the provision and policy of local authorities across the UK varies enormously. There are also always changes taking place in both the kind of provision available in your area and different government policies and attitudes to education.

The first main thing to bear to mind is that what educationally suits one child with FASD may not be appropriate for another FASD affected child, even within the same biological family.

Secondly, what may be right school-wise for a child when they are 5 may not be the right school or environment for them when they are 8. One child began school in a mainstream school with support, then moved into a special unit within mainstream. At 8 they transferred to a special needs school, before later being home-schooled and then at 16 going to the local Higher Education (16+) college and taking a 2 year course on living & independence skills for young adults with learning disabilities.

As with every other area of life with a child affected by FASD, expectations have to change. Do not expect to attend the same primary school then the same senior school, then off to university / higher education. Your child might achieve this, but many children with FASD will not. The important thing is to keep aware of local provision, to re-assess your child's educational needs and then do your best to ensure these are met, which is often not an easy task.

Once you suspect your child is affected by FASD or they are formally diagnosed, inform the school. Inform your child's class teacher first. Every school has a SENCO (special educational needs co-ordinator). Ask the class teacher who the SENCO is – in smaller schools it is often the headteacher – and ask the class teacher if you can meet with them and the SENCO. If your child is in senior school, it may well be worthwhile asking for the Head of Year to be attend the meeting.

For Looked After Children, additional support is also available from the authority's Virtual School and within school itself there should be a Designated Teacher with responsibility for the all children in the school who are Looked After.

It can be helpful as well to contact your local education authority's special educational needs team and seek their advice on what support is available. Some children will qualify for an EHCP (Education, Health & Care Plan) but not all, however the local team will be able to advise you and give you information about other sources of local support available to you.

Some children will qualify for an assessment by an Educational Psychologist in school; ask the school if they will refer your child for such an assessment.

If there are other professionals, such as speech & language therapists or physiotherapist involved in your child's life ask them if they would visit your child in school and assess them in the school setting. Inform the school of the other professional's name and contact details and advise school that you have given permission for them to see your child in school. The therapist can then give school as well as yourself some advice on how to help your child.

Sometimes it can be overwhelming or frustrating dealing with school, especially if your child is unhappy or you feel the provision is not meeting your child's needs. Do not hesitate to seek the help and support of others, including charities, such as The FASD Trust, who are there to support you and provide you with information. There is also in each local education authority a parents' mediation service, often provided by the local parent partnership, who will be able to send someone independent to attend meetings with you and calmly explain, on your behalf, your concerns.

With the right support, children with FASD can learn and can achieve their potential; it is often achieved though via their own individual route and, as one parent phrased it, "My daughter is highly successful in her own world."

17 Becoming independent

Parents will find the transition from child to adult frustrating and difficult. They see the support package they have spent years fighting for and building up being removed overnight as the child reaches 18. Whilst we are working towards better support for adults with FASD, the provision remains at the time of writing as very patchy and fragmented and carers often find they are frustratingly passed around from agency to agency to access the support they need.

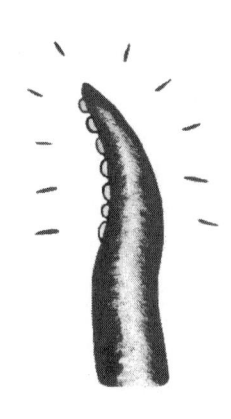

Parenting any young adult is very challenging and parenting the FASD child is extra-challenging. FASD affects an individual's ability to live independently throughout their lives. Nearly 80 per cent of adults with FASD do not live independently.

FASD is an invisible disability. People in the 'real world' do not see the disability, especially when the person has a normal IQ and good verbal skills, which mask the underlying deficits in executive function. Affected adults are often expected to live completely independently once they leave school.

The group most at risk are the young adults looked after by a local authority who are expected to leave care with their peers and then manage alone with little additional support. Unfortunately, these young people are also unsophisticated and naïve and lack the basic skills to cope with independent living. If the child you are caring for is in the care of the local authority consider exploring with them the option of the child remaining in your care for longer than the normal care-leaving age. This takes a lot of forward planning as discussions with the local authority always take time.

As a child approaches their teenage years, it is time to start planning ahead for adulthood and to begin teaching life skills in earnest. It will take some children several years to master even the basics. Early planning however does not mean that the child will become independent early. Expect your child to become independent much later than other children. If possible, plan to have your child live at home with you until their late 20s or even mid-30s. Once again supervision is the key and hopefully, all those early years of laying good foundations will come to fruition.

Most adults with FASD will need a lot of help to meet the more routine demands of work and home. Areas where help will be needed include employment, money management, housing, and social skills. Many require close daily supervision to help them make essential day-to-day decisions and keep themselves safe. Always remember that the dependence of the affected adult on the community around them started at birth for these young people and this support becomes more essential as they approach adult life.

It is important to change the focus from an exaggerated expectation on **independence** to one of **interdependence**. A local supportive community is important for everyone, but it is essential for people with FASD. They need a strong circle of support made up of family members, mentors, social workers, agency support workers, and others who understand the realities and limitations of FASD.

Housing is a major issue for persons with an FASD. Homelessness is a major risk. Many adults with FASD alienate their families or friends because of their unpredictable behaviour. Living in shelters, sleeping on the sofa at friends' homes for a few days at a time or living on the street are likely to be at best disorientating, and at worst life-threatening to someone affected by FASD. It is therefore essential to integrate appropriate housing into any transition plan. These young people need a consistent, predictable and calm environment which is usually hard to find.

Housing is going to be dependent on your child's level of understanding and level of difficulties, as well as your personal family circumstances and choices. Families with means sometimes purchase a residence for their FASD-affected child, or pay rent indefinitely on an apartment or a bedsit. Other families have explored options for supported housing, shared housing, a residential home for the disabled or adapting their own home. One family even purchased a caravan which sits in their garden in order to give their son some independence. Group homes tailored to persons with FASD do not currently exist. Group homes for individuals with mental disabilities or mental illness may be an option, but they can be a poor fit for people with an FASD, who often function at a higher level than their housemates or have different needs.

Even when the affected adult has a job and can afford to pay some rent, their ability to live independently is dependent on their parents, or other person, to act as the 'external brain'. This will involve reminding the person with FASD to eat regularly, pay the rent on time, pay the utility bills and obey the rules established by the landlord.

When you are thinking about your child moving out there are also other practical considerations. Can they cook? Are they able to safely operate an oven? Can they do their own washing? Can they buy their own food? If not, can you 'buy in' external support, such as a weekly cleaner or someone to do the ironing? Is there a good college nearby which teaches life skills to young people with disabilities? What job will they go on to do? There are agencies that work with disabled teenagers to help find them work, but unfortunately, all too often, the emphasis is on access for those with physical rather than mental disabilities. Look around too for the support available from both the charitable, religious and statutory sector in terms of buddy schemes, befrienders or volunteers who visit the vulnerable.

Driving is another issue. It will depend on your child's level of ability as to whether or not you feel it is safe for them to learn to drive. Remember, at the wheel, a driver has to cope with a lot of different information, the speed of the car, the speed of the oncoming traffic, the weather, unexpected behaviour from pedestrians or cyclists and distractions from others. The FASD adult who finds all information difficult to process may not be able to cope with the level of executive functioning necessary to be safe at the wheel.

Explore other ways of giving your child 'independence' in terms of transport. Can you get the local authority to pay for their transport to college in an escorted minibus or taxi service? Do you live near a good bus or train route that takes them directly to their destination? Do you have friends whose teenagers can drive, whom you trust, and who could give your child a lift? For parents it is always a difficult balance between allowing a young adult to participate in life and keeping them and others safe. They need to be given freedom, but in a way that is supervised.

People with an FASD can either find it difficult to access financial benefits or not realise they are entitled to any such support. However, although each successive Government may changes the rules or names of benefits, there is financial support available. It is strongly recommended that parents or carers, including foster carers, contact the Department of Work and Pensions, their local job centre and the local council to explore what benefits are currently available for which they can apply.

There is a current trend towards 'personal payments' where the parent or young person receives a lump sum which they can use to purchase external help. Disability Living Allowance is also currently available and is not means-tested; we advise all parents to apply as the criteria is not dependent on any specific diagnosis, but is about the fact that your child needs more support to do tasks than other children of the same age.

It is easier for a young person who has been in receipt of childhood financial support to then transition to appropriate adult benefits and services, rather than having to 'fight' to gain financial support for a young adult who could be perceived as 'work-shy' rather than having a genuine condition and difficulties.

Many parents worry about their child being drawn into drugs, alcohol and crime. First of all, research has consistently shown that children learn their alcohol-drinking habits from their parents or primary carers, so ensure that you are giving them a positive role model. Secondly, ensure your child has hobbies and interests away from the pub and away from parties and other social situations where drugs and alcohol could be offered to them. Try to include some activities that are physical, such as swimming or horse-riding. Now they are now older consider exploring options for activities which involve 'risk' such as abseiling or rock-climbing at a properly supervised centre. Thirdly ensure that your previous building-up of contacts and friendships around your child means they are mixing with people who understand them and will steer them away from unsafe behaviour and situations.

Unfortunately, none of us can totally wrap our children up in cotton wool, so you will need to talk to your child and teach them to say 'no' if they are offered any alcohol or drugs. Hopefully, a mixture of keeping them occupied elsewhere, the right relationships, discreet supervision and some preteaching on saying 'no' will all combine to keep them safe.

It is possible for those with FASD to hold down a job, though their employer and colleagues will need to understand their difficulties and disability. If they have clear routines and supervision, we find many with FASD can be successful in the world of work. (We find that some struggle to work full-time, as they do tire easily.) Alternatively, use your child's hobby, such as photography or dancing, and turn that into a profession. (One young woman in her 20s is now a successful dance teacher; another young man a great photographer.) Just as when they were younger, they will need trustworthy people around them, who can look after the financial and administrative side of any business.

Having FASD does not mean you are barred from having a fulfilling relationship or being a parent. We are aware of cases where, given the right support from their partner, some adults with FASD are parenting successfully. The FASD Trust has a range of leaflets available for carers and young people that teach about sex, sexuality and relationships in a way that is accessible for those with FASD.

At the time of writing, we are starting to question and lobby those responsible for the lack of services and support provided for adults with FASD. Statutory provision is too patchy and based on individual cases. The best thing to do is to assess your child's strengths and define their needs – then go out and fight for the specific support they need to enjoy and participate in life safely and to the full.

18   Final word to parents

Parenting a child with FASD can be exhausting, challenging, frustrating and, at times, totally overwhelming. Indeed, one mother, whose previous role was managing a children's home, said that caring for her child with FASD was the hardest role she had ever undertaken!

However, parenting these children can also be the most rewarding and fulfilling role you have ever undertaken. These children can be endearing, funny, creative - a whole long list of positives!

Unfortunately, the tendency when caring for children affected by FASD can be to focus constantly on what the child cannot achieve, on which areas the child needs additional support, on constantly pushing to achieve "normality", to make the child "fit in" and to "cure" everything. (It is does not help either when you are completing endless government forms and attending constant appointments with professionals who all ask about the things your child cannot achieve.)

It is therefore important to remind yourself what your child can achieve, to work out their strengths and to highlight them to the child, as well as yourself. Many of these children have low self-esteem due to being constantly told "no" and "you cannot". Try and re-phrase things when talking to your child; tell them what you want them to do, rather than what you don't want them to do, so you are speaking out positive requests rather than negative commands.

One dad stood his child in front of the mirror each morning and said, "You are brilliant, clever and fabulous." One day, someone asked the child, "Who are you?" to which the child promptly replied, "Brilliant, clever and fabulous." Can your child articulate the things about themselves and their character which is positive?

Children with FASD do eventually master some skills, but probably later than other children, which means you have to learn to keep encouraging your child in a consistent, but relaxed way. Your child will pick up on your stress levels and their anxiety about a task and their ability to achieve it will increase, thus decreasing their chance of success.

It is also extremely important that you take some time to care for yourself and, if you are in a relationship, in maintaining it. It is often hard work - or impossible - to arrange a babysitter, which is where you have to be as creative with maintaining your relationship as in supporting your child. Instead of evening dinner together, can you arrange to have a special lunch with each other while the kids are in school? Can you take a morning off work and spend it together rather than a night out? If your kids do actually sleep on a morning, get up early and have a quiet breakfast together.

It can be exhausting juggling kids, work, multiple appointments and housework. If you can afford it, consider a cleaner to help around the house. As one person phrased it, "£10 an hour for a cleaner is cheaper than £200 an hour for a psychiatrist - or divorce lawyer." We find many people have relatives who cannot cope caring for the FASD affected child in the family, but they are a great support on a practical level around their home. Do you have any close friends or relatives who could do a load of ironing for you or cut the grass or run the vacuum over the living room once a week?

Being part of a support group can often help on the practical front too as there will be a wider pool of people who you can get to know and trust and then who can assist you with perhaps setting up your own local FASD baby-sitting circle.

Ensure you take time to care for yourself both health-wise and in terms of giving yourself a rest from focusing constantly on your parenting duties. You don't have to take up an expensive new hobby - it might just be an hour spent in the local library quietly reading a book, go to the hairdresser, go out for a walk or a run or bike ride, sit in the back garden. If at work, go out with colleagues at lunchtime rather than sitting at your desk. Whatever you do, it is important though, for your own sanity, to have these moments when you have "space" for you.

Finally, the most important thing to remember is that first and foremost you are your child's parent. Your child will have lots of difficulties, needs and issues, but their primary need is for a parent who loves them unconditionally and is simply there.

We see lots of parents who are so stressed and focused on the negative and desperately trying to fix everything that they have somehow forgotten to simply be a parent and to enjoy their children.

So, what do you enjoy doing together as a family unit? What are the "family memories" you are building with your child? Everyone squashed on the sofa on a rainy Saturday eating popcorn watching a film? Everyone in the back garden on a sunny Saturday having a water fight in the paddling pool? Sitting on the beach on a summer's day digging a big hole? Everyone curled up together on squashy cushions looking at the big picture book?

Ultimately, as Simon wrote in the Foreword to this book there is no "right" or "wrong" way to parent children with FASD. We hope though that some of the pointers in this book will help you as you continue your personal journey of parenting a child affected by FASD.

Further Information

The FASD Trust, the national leading charity supporting those affected by FASD. They run support groups and other services across the UK.
www.fasdtrust.co.uk

The FASD Trust also hosts an on-line forum specifically for parents & carers where posts / queries can be made anonymously and advice / support sought from other parents & carers. It is also a useful source of information on events and activities.
http://fasdtrust.healthunlocked.com/

The FASD Trust can also be found on social media
Facebook Page: www.facebook.com/FASDTrust
Facebook Group:
www.facebook.com/groups/51551662034
Twitter: Follow them at #FASD_Trust

Printed in Great Britain
by Amazon